Cambridge Elements ≡

Elements in Law, Economics and Politics

Series Editor in Chief
Carmine Guerriero, *University of Bologna*

Series Co-Editors
Alessandro Riboni, *École Polytechnique*
Jillian Grennan, *Duke University, Fuqua School of Business*
Petros Sekeris, *Montpellier Business School*

REFORM FOR SALE

A Common Agency Model with Moral Hazard Frictions

Perrin Lefebvre
University of Namur

David Martimort
Toulouse School of Economics

CAMBRIDGE
UNIVERSITY PRESS

CAMBRIDGE
UNIVERSITY PRESS

Shaftesbury Road, Cambridge CB2 8EA, United Kingdom

One Liberty Plaza, 20th Floor, New York, NY 10006, USA

477 Williamstown Road, Port Melbourne, VIC 3207, Australia

314–321, 3rd Floor, Plot 3, Splendor Forum, Jasola District Centre, New Delhi – 110025, India

103 Penang Road, #05–06/07, Visioncrest Commercial, Singapore 238467

Cambridge University Press is part of Cambridge University Press & Assessment, a department of the University of Cambridge.

We share the University's mission to contribute to society through the pursuit of education, learning and research at the highest international levels of excellence.

www.cambridge.org
Information on this title: www.cambridge.org/9781009285582
DOI: 10.1017/9781009285605

© Perrin Lefebvre and David Martimort 2023

First published 2023

A catalogue record for this publication is available from the British Library.

ISBN 978-1-009-28558-2 Paperback
ISSN 2732-4931 (online)
ISSN 2732-4923 (print)

Additional resources for this publication at www.cambridge.org/Martimort_Online appendix.

Reform for Sale
A Common Agency Model with Moral Hazard Frictions

Elements in Law, Economics and Politics

DOI: 10.1017/9781009285605
First published online: February 2023

Perrin Lefebvre
University of Namur
David Martimort
Toulouse School of Economics

Author for correspondence: David Martimort, david.martimort@tse-fr.eu

Abstract: Lobbying competition is viewed as a delegated common agency game under moral hazard. Several interest groups try to influence a policy-maker who exerts effort to increase the probability that a reform be implemented. With no restriction on the space of contribution schedules, all equilibria perfectly reflect the principals' preferences over alternatives. As a result, lobbying competition reaches efficiency. Unfortunately, such equilibria require that the policy-maker pays an interest group when the latter is hurt by the reform. When payments remain non-negative, inducing effort requires leaving a moral hazard rent to the decision maker. Contributions schedules no longer reflect the principals' preferences, and the unique equilibrium is inefficient. Free-riding across congruent groups arises and the set of groups active at equilibrium is endogenously derived. Allocative efficiency and redistribution of the aggregate surplus is linked altogether and both depend on the set of active principals, as well as on the group size.

Keywords: Lobbying, multiprincipals, pluralistic politics, common agency, moral hazard

ISBNs: 9781009285582 (PB), 9781009285605 (OC)
ISSNs: 2732-4931 (online), 2732-4923 (print)

Contents

Further online supplementary material can be accessed at www.cambridge.org/Martimort_Online appendix

1 Introduction

There exists by now a large consensus among political scientists and economists on the fact that political decision-makers are best viewed as facing a fragmented front of political stimuli emanating from *multiple principals*. This pluralistic view of politics, which was touched upon earlier on by Bentley (1908) and Truman (1951) and certainly culminated in the work of Dahl (1961), applies at various layers of the overall decision-making process.

To illustrate, Congress and the Presidency might have different preferences on policy goals. Yet, both the Legislative and the Executive branches of the government influence how bureaucratic agencies run and implement various regulations (Epstein and O'Halloran, 1997, 1999; Snyder and Weingast, 2000). Similarly, Legislators are generally responsive to several interest groups that offer campaign contributions or even bribes in exchange of their services in the political arena (Grossman and Helpman, 1994, 2001; Spiller and Urbiztondo, 1994). Finally, the multiprincipal nature of the government trickles down to the mere implementation of regulatory policies. There, oversight by multiple agencies is indeed the rule rather than the exception (Moe, 1981, 1989; Baron, 1985; Wilson, 1989; Dixit, 1996; Martimort, 1996).

A Brief Critical Overview of Common Agency Models and Politics

Following the seminal work of Bernheim and Whinston (1986a, 1986b), those situations have been modeled as *common agency games*. In a nutshell, a common agency model works as follows. Several principals (interest groups, public bodies) noncooperatively design contribution schedules to influence a single policy-maker. This common agent chooses which offers to accept and which decision should be taken. The decision may be a vector of regulated prices on domestic and international markets or whether a particular reform should be implemented or not. The schedule offered by each principal stipulates how much that principal is ready to pay for a given decision. Bernheim and Whinston (1986b) demonstrated that the set of equilibria of this three-stage game may be quite large. To refine within this equilibrium set, they observed that each principal has always in his best-response correspondence a *truthful* contribution schedule. A *truthful* contribution schedule perfectly reflects the principal's preferences over alternative actions.[1] Truthful contributions make de facto the

---

[1] Technically, truthful contributions as defined by Bernheim (1986b) either perfectly reflect the principal's preferences among actions or stipulate a null contribution to the agent. Yet, the subsequent literature has generally focused on the first meaning, which conveys most of the economic intuitions at play.

policy decision-maker *residual claimant* for the decision made. As it is so for all principals, the agent fully internalizes the whole welfare of principals at any *truthful equilibrium*. The public decision maximizes the aggregate payoff of the grand coalition formed by the contributing principals and the common agent and thus ends up being always efficient. Although different truthful equilibria may entail different distributions of the overall surplus among the principals and their common agent, the policy chosen is welfare maximizing and thus essentially unique under weak conditions of strict concavity.

This model of the political process yields a striking and, in a sense, quite surprising result. According to this so-called *Pluralistic View of Politics*, the political process is *frictionless*. This *Chicago-like* approach of politics thus suggests that free entry in the political arena together with some form of perfect competition among interest groups would definitively ensure social-welfare maximization. And this even if policy decision-makers are not subject to any formal constraint on behavior and conduct.

This conclusion is clearly at odds with reality for at least three reasons. First, because it does not generate transaction costs of any sort, the standard common agency approach cannot explain why some groups form and are active players in the political arena, whereas others remain inactive.

Second, and for the same reason, the paradigm is silent on the boundaries of interest groups. Indeed, the common agency approach leaves no room for active groups to build coalition or even merge to leverage their influence (unless such merger allows to better extract the agent's rent). Indeed, in any case, the decision implemented is always efficient and thus remains unchanged. By the same token, the paradigm fails to explain why individual players should ever join groups instead of acting as separate principals on their own; a point forcefully emphasized by Mallard (2014) and Martimort (2018). In other words, the paradigm has been developed without any consideration for the free-riding problem that Olson (1965) stressed as a key determinant of collective action problems. As a model of political economy, this weakness is actually a serious blow.

Third, the common agency model also treats separately redistributive and allocative issues. Again, because the decision chosen by the common agent is always efficient, the distribution of welfare among interest groups has no impact whatsoever on this decision and vice versa. As a model of political economy, this feature is at best unpleasant. If anything, political economy should precisely be concerned by the link between the policies chosen on the one hand and the payoff distribution they induce among stakeholders on the other hand. Indeed, the common agency model under complete information beautifully derives the feasible redistributions of the surplus among the interest groups which are assumed to actively influence the policy-maker, but, again, this redistribution has no impact on the decision which ends up being taken.

Moral Hazard as a Source of Contractual Frictions

In this Element, we take stock of the lessons of the existing common agency literature but modify this basic framework in a crucial direction. We explicitly introduce an agency problem between political principals and the policy-maker under the form of moral hazard. Moral hazard is a quite natural assumption in the framework of political delegation as it has been argued forcefully by several political scientists.[2]

Our running example throughout the Element has a decision-maker exerting a nonobservable effort that affects the probability that a reform be passed. Interest groups can favor or oppose the reform. Interest groups aim at influencing the decision-maker by means of contribution schedules that stipulate a payment to the decision-maker for each possible outcome: typically, whether the reform passes or fails. Although the principals' contributions can be made contingent on outcomes, they cannot depend explicitly on the action taken by the decision-maker. For example, contribution schedules cannot depend on whether the policy-maker in charge has worked hard or not to convince other politicians or the rest of citizens of the benefits of his decision.

This agency problem potentially may generate contractual frictions. Those frictions shape the interest groups' incentives to become active or not and, if active, to engage in coalition building with other groups if it helps leveraging collective influence. In other words, contractual frictions are key not only to explain the landscape of active interest groups but also to provide the missing link between the redistributive and the allocative sides of the political process that the previous complete information literature unfortunately failed to recognize.

Moral Hazard Might Not Always Suffice to Generate Contractual Frictions

Our analysis of moral hazard in common agency lobbying games starts by considering the most general set of feasible contributions given the informational constraint faced by interest groups. In this most unrestricted contracting scenario, each of those principals is able to offer payments contingent for

---

[2] For instance, Kiewiet and McCubbins (1991) argue that delegation of political decision-making from elected political majorities to standing committees and subcommittees within each chamber creates a conflict between what those majorities want and the policies that end up being implemented.

all possible outcomes of the political process. For instance, payments to the decision-maker only depend on whether a reform passes or fails. In this unrestricted contracting environment, making a risk-neutral decision-maker residual claimant for the interest group's benefits of the chosen policy is always a best response for this principal whatever contributions other competing groups are actually offering. This well-known result from the principal-agent literature carries thus over in a noncooperative context where groups compete for influence. At equilibrium, contribution schedules align each group's preferences over alternatives with those of the common agent. Contributions are again *truthful* in this moral hazard scenario.

However, the meaning of *truthfulness* slightly differs from what is commonly understood in the complete information scenario. In contrast with Bernheim and Whinston (1986b)'s original work, contributions now perfectly reflect the principals' relative preferences among *outcomes* and not among the actions that the agent could entertain. In a moral hazard environment with a standard *full support* assumption, all outcomes are feasible with some probability whatever the common agent's action. To illustrate, a reform can pass or fail with some probability and although this probability may change with the policy-maker's effort, there always remains uncertainty on final outcomes. From a technical viewpoint, the issue of extending the contribution schedules for outcomes which are not reached on the equilibrium path thus disappears in our framework. It is not necessary to impose any equilibrium refinement to justify truthfulness. Equilibrium schedules *must* satisfy this property. Compared with the case of complete information, the introduction of moral hazard significantly increases the predictive power of the common agency model.

Yet, even in a moral hazard environment, the main lesson of the common agency literature pertains. The risk-neutral decision-maker again ends up being made residual claimant by all principals for all consequences of his or her action. Accordingly, all interest groups are active at equilibrium, and the agent chooses an action which maximizes the payoff of the grand coalition he or she forms with those active principals. The political process remains frictionless; thereby confirming the main takeaway of the *Pluralistic Approach of Politics*. Moral hazard alone is not enough to challenge this efficiency view of competition in politics.

Nonnegative Contributions and Frictions

To get some meaningful contractual frictions, we have to consider a more restricted contracting environment where interest groups can no longer make the agent residual claimant for their own objectives. In fact, the residual claimancy argument relies on the possibility for the policy-maker to compensate the interest group in case it is hurt by the decision taken: an unpalatable conclusion. The policy-maker could indeed always have the option to renege on an earlier agreement with an interest group and he will certainly do so whenever asked to compensate the group if some political outcome that hurts this group realizes.

A contrario, consider thus the scenario where interest groups only pay for the outcome that pleases them the most. Imposing this additional condition that transfers should be nonnegative generates meaningful agency frictions that render the picture of the game of influence much more realistic. To study in fine details these frictions, we distinguish two cases. In the first one, all principals have *congruent preferences* and are pleased when the reform succeeds. To illustrate, two interest groups are congruent if they want to push toward the adoption of the reform. In the second scenario, the groups have *conflicting* preferences and compete head-to-head for the policy-maker's services.

With congruent preferences, all interest groups prefer that the policy-maker exerts more effort toward implementing the reform. This effort becomes thus a *public good* and interest groups contribute to its provision by independently rewarding the common agent. Now, each principal enjoys only form a fraction of the aggregate benefit of a reform but, under a noncooperative behavior, has to pay for the full agency cost (as it resorts from the analysis) of implementing it. Because principals are not cooperating in designing contributions, *free riding* in the provision of incentives follows. This leads to a familiar under-provision of the agent's effort and the likelihood of a reform decreases accordingly.

This negative externality provides the key ingredient to explain entry into the political process. When an interest group's valuation for the reform is less than the corresponding agency cost it bears from its relationship with the decision-maker, its equilibrium contribution is null. Those principals do not contribute and remain out of the political process. The policy chosen by the common agent in equilibrium reflects thus only the preferences of the principals who are the most willing to intervene. This effect is crucial. It gives us a link between the *allocative efficiency* of the policy choice, the *endogenous structure* of active groups, and the *distribution of surplus* across those groups.

Importantly, heterogeneity is key to explain that some interest groups do not act. If all congruent interest groups are alike, they all intervene even though the political outcome still reflects the existing *free riding* among them and the likelihood of a reform is inefficiently low. This shows that redistribution of the benefits of the reform among interest groups has a *nonneutral* impact on the policy chosen.

The extent of the free-riding problem and its determinants, namely, the size of a group and the heterogeneity among its members, is now a fundamental driver of the game of influence. While adding new members to a group, by increasing the aggregate valuation, strengthens this group's influence, size in itself decreases a group's ability to exert influence. That is, for a given aggregate valuation, smaller groups will be more efficient than larger ones. In addition, groups with more homogeneous members tend to be more effective than groups whose members are more diversely affected by the policy.

Those frictions in the interaction among principals also modify the scope for coalition building among groups. Under unrestricted contracting, all the collective gains are exhausted via groups' competition. Coalition building can only be valuable when it helps in reducing the rent the agent can extract from groups' competition, while it has no impact on the policy decision. By contrast, free riding provides groups with an incentive to merge in order to cooperatively design their contributions. Such a joint design of contribution not only affects the distribution of the collective gains, but also the eventual decision and therefore the collective gain achieved from the policy process.

In the case of conflicting principals, most of the aforementioned features carry over although details change. In particular, conflicting principals may face different agency costs and evaluate in quite different ways the cost of entering the political arena. The result is that head-to-head competition between conflicting groups is more likely to induce a very asymmetric political landscape; the weaker group remaining outside the political arena.

Organization of the Element

Section 2 reviews the relevant literature. Section 3 presents our model of a political process leading to adopting or not a reform. This problem is viewed as a delegated common agency game under moral hazard. In Section 4, we derive the properties of equilibria when principals are unrestricted in the contribution schedules they may use. In Section 5, we introduce the nonnegativity constraints on payments. We analyze two important benchmarks for the rest of the analysis: the cooperative outcome and the scenario of *intrinsic common agency game*. We deduce from there the moral hazard frictions that affect the political process. Section 6 develops the case of congruent principals, whereas Section 7 deals with the scenario of conflicting interests. Section 8 analyzes the incentives of interest groups to merge to leverage their common influence. Section 9 briefly concludes. Proofs are relegated to Appendix A. In addition, Appendix B develops etc. an alternative scenario where the source of the agency frictions is the agent's risk aversion.

2 Literature Review

This Element has both a political economy and a methodological motivation. Our review of the extant literature reflects those two concerns and we now cover each in turn, although sometimes where we set the boundary between the two is a matter of tastes.

On the Political Economy Front

Over the past few decades, applications of the common agency model to various political economy contexts have flourished as exemplified by the work of Aidt (1998), Dixit, Grossman, and Helpman (1997), Rama and Tabellini (1998), Besley and Coate (2001), Grossman and Helpman (1994, 2001), Helpman and Persson (2001), and Yu (2005), among many others. Mallard (2014) and Martimort (2018) have written extensive surveys of this literature but have also stressed some of the limits of this approach. As the common agency model became extensively used as a description of political influence, getting a more realistic picture of the political process has been high on the research agenda.

In an attempt to reconcile redistributive and efficiency concerns, Dixit, Grossman, and Helpman (1997) have departed from the quasi-linear world inherited from Bernheim and Whinston (1986b) by introducing income effects. Unfortunately, the efficiency property of the truthful equilibria of the corresponding common agency games is preserved. In other words, redistributive concerns alone are unable to generate any frictions in the political process.

A key aspect of realism is certainly asymmetric information. Assuming asymmetric information on the agent's side and ex post contracting, Laussel and Le Breton (1998b), Le Breton and Salanié (2003), Martimort (2007b, 2008), and Martimort (2018) have also analyzed, as we do hereafter, the magnitude of the free-riding problem among interest groups. Putting an agency problem at the core of the analysis, be it induced by hidden information or hidden action, gives a fresh look at the Olsonian program of finding the determinants of groups' collective action.[3] Olson identified free riding among actors

---

[3] In this Element, as in Olson (1965) and most of the literature on collective action, the vocable *group* applies as well to a set of individuals with some common interest, and to some organized structure able to develop its own strategy of political influence. The way these concepts overlap or not depends arguably on the size of the group. In a small group, each member could as well act on his own. But in a larger group, and especially when dealing with contracts made to a policy-maker, organization seems a prerequisite of any action. This second aspect is best referred to as the *formation* of groups, while when all groups (or members of a group) are assumed to be already able do device their own contract, as in this Element, the situation is better described in terms of *interactions*.

with similar preferences as a major impediment to collective action. We will argue in Section 6 that this free-riding problem can be endogenized as coming from a contractual externality among contributors. Moreover, *free riding* is not enough *alone* to justify that an interest group fails to intervene. This failure is also linked to the existence of other competing groups. The whole landscape of competitors of an interest group matters to determine whether the latter intervenes or not.

In this respect, Lefebvre and Martimort (2020) have offered a model that explicitly integrates a group-formation stage in the analysis of the lobbying process. Forming an active group is actually a collective action problem that is made difficult by the fact that individual members have private information on their own marginal benefit of the group's influence on policy. Such private information is the source of a free-riding problem which now bites within groups. This free riding might undermine their influence in the political process, sometimes up to the point of eschewing any influence at all.[4] Asymmetric information on the principals' side in common agency model has also been studied by Martimort and Moreira (2010) and Lima and Moreira (2014) who argue that it is a major source of inefficiency.

Still assuming that decision-makers hold private information, Martimort and Stole (2018) have also shown that, if the principals' preferences are close to each other, all principals contribute in equilibrium; confirming thereby one of our results in corollary 1 in Section 6. This latter paper can indeed be viewed as the adverse selection version of the present work, with many results mirroring those found in this Element, especially in Section 6, under moral hazard. There also, an interest group intervenes if its benefit of doing so exceeds the corresponding agency costs. Of course, with asymmetric information, agency costs are of a different nature. As a result, marginal contributions are no longer truthful. Contributions offered by a group have to be discounted below its (marginal) willingness to pay to reflect the group's difficulty in solving the asymmetric information problem vis-à-vis the policy-maker. This point was made in various contexts by Martimort and Semenov (2007b, 2008) and Martimort and Stole (2018).

In the standard Chicago view of the political process pushed forward by Peltzman (1976) and later on by Becker (1983, 1985), the influence function which describes how interest groups exert pressure on a policy-maker is ad hoc and given at the outset. In Becker (1983, 1985), for instance, this function may not only depend on whether a group favors or not more spending, but also on the group size. The common agency approach makes progress on that front

---

[4] See also Leaver and Makris (2006) for a model with similar intuitions.

insofar as actual competition among interest groups is now explicitly modeled as a menu auction where interest groups design contribution schedules to influence the decision-maker. Of course, because this approach also implies that the equilibrium is efficient, it fails to offer a link between the size of the group and its political pressure. We will argue in Section 6 that the common agency approach, when conveniently amended to account for agency costs, is able to endogenize pressure functions and link them to group size.

Finally, this Element also significantly differs from most of the applied common agency literature because the subset of interest groups which intervene is not specified a priori but instead derived from the equilibrium analysis. To fill this gap of the earlier literature, Mitra (1999) was the first to introduce exogenous fixed costs of entering the political process, a route which was then also taken by Martimort and Semenov (2007a) and Bombardini (2008) among others. Entry costs somewhat endogenize the set of active principals and thus offer a direct link between the policy chosen in response to those active groups and the distribution of surplus. In this Element, the same link arises but this exogenous fixed cost is now replaced by agency costs which are endogenous to the problem.

On the Methodological Front

Several contributions dealing with moral hazard, most noticeably those of Bernheim and Whinston (1986a) in a general agency framework and Dixit (1996) in a political economy environment, have focused on intrinsic common agency games. Under intrinsic common agency, the agent accepts or refuses all contracts at once.[5] Although possibly attractive to model political settings like bureaucratic oversight by multiple committees or split control of a regulated firm between different regulatory bodies, those models seem less relevant to capture issues related to the competition among various interest groups willing to influence a common policy-maker and attract his favors. In sharp contrast, this Element analyzes the issue of delegated common agency in a moral hazard environment.

In this respect, this Element is tangentially related to a broader literature on competitive equilibrium in insurance markets plagued with moral hazard (Pauly, 1974; Helpman and Laffont, 1975; Hellwig, 1983; Arnott and Stiglitz, 1991; Bisin and Guaitoli, 2004; Attar and Chassagnon, 2009; Attar et al., 2019). There also multiple principals post contracts to attract an agent.

---

[5] See also Fraysse (1993), Peters (2003), Attar, Piaser, and Porteiro (2007a, 2007b), Martimort and Stole (2012), and Gottlieb and Moreira (2021).

This agent exerts a 0–1 effort; a feature which introduces a fundamental non-convexity into the model. The issues that are investigated by this literature are mostly the constrained-efficiency properties of competitive equilibria, whether exclusive contracting is feasible and its consequences and, finally, the role of off-path contracts to sustain equilibrium allocations. Those concerns are not really relevant in our political economy context that has a finite number of strategic principals acting without any of those being able to enforce any exclusivity clause.

As mentioned in the introduction, the truthfulness criterion used in the complete information literature is actually a refinement of the equilibrium set. Contributions stipulating threats for unexpected changes in the agent's decision make it easy to sustain many other equilibrium outcomes. Some of these outcomes are possibly not efficient. This point was made in Martimort (2007) and Chiesa and Denicolò (2009) among others. Although found attractive for applications, the truthfulness criterion has thus been questioned in terms of its foundations. Under complete information, it seems hard to a priori preclude the use of simple forcing contracts, in which case, a plethora of (inefficient) equilibria emerges. In this respect, Kirchsteiger and Prat (2001) defined *natural* equilibria as associated with forcing contracts. By running an experiment, those authors showed that, under complete information, players tend to play natural rather than truthful equilibria. Note also that forcing contracts may significantly save on menu costs. In a complete information private common agency context where each principal is only affected by a subset of the agent's actions, Chiesa and Denicolò (2009) have also shown that truthful contracts might even be Pareto-dominated from the principals' viewpoint.

Our analysis of the case of unrestricted contracting demonstrates how truthfulness arises there as a best-response property at all equilibria. It is thus no longer a refinement criterion. Laussel and Le Breton (1998a) have also obtained a similar result in a model with hidden information on a parameter of the agent's utility function and ex ante contracting. Incentive constraints then pin down the slope of the contribution schedule at any equilibrium decision. With ex ante contracting, efficiency is still achieved for any realization of the underlying uncertainty. However, truthful contributions might also be used off equilibrium to compute the agent's reservation payoffs if he deviates and refuses one of the proposed contracts. Those extensions have thus a nontrivial redistributive impact since they determine how much each principal can extract from the common agent and thus how much he gets at equilibrium. This issue is also investigated in Martimort and Stole (2009) under the assumption of ex post contracting, that is, when the agent already knows his type before contracting. Working in a delegated common agency model with moral hazard avoids those arbitrary extensions since every political outcome has some nonzero probability on the equilibrium path when a standard assumption of full support is made.

Lastly, Bernheim and Whinston (1986b) have demonstrated that truthful equilibria have also the additional property that they are immune to deviations by coalitions of principals which are themselves robust to further deviations by sub-coalitions. Furusawa and Konishi (2011) have extended the notion of coalition-proofness when entry is also a strategic decision for principals. Yet, we will show in Section 8 that this quite demanding criterion does not exhaust incentives for coalition building with moral hazard frictions.

3 The Model

Preferences

There are n interest groups (sometimes referred to as *the principals*) in the economy. Those groups are indexed by $i \in N = \{0, 1, \ldots, n\}$.

A policy-maker (the agent) exerts an action e which affects the probability that a reform is enacted. One may think of this reform as, for instance, opening trade barriers and adopting free trade or tightening existing regulatory standards. For most of this Element, we thus focus on a 0–1 political decision. This assumption simplifies the analysis and allows to get clear results which have nevertheless a broader generality.[6] To fix ideas, one can think of e as the effort and resource that the policy-maker devotes to convince other policy-makers but also voters that the reform should be adopted. To simplify notations, we identify e with the probability that the reform passes. With complementary probability $1 - e$, the status quo instead prevails.

Interest group i thus gets an expected payoff given by

$$V_i = \mathbb{E}\left(\tilde{S}_i - \tilde{t}_i | e\right), \tag{3.1}$$

where $\mathbb{E}(\cdot | e)$ denotes the expectation operator with respect to the distribution of political outcomes induced by effort e, and $\tilde{S}_i$ and $\tilde{t}_i$ are random variables that stand for the benefit that accrues to group i and the payment it makes to the decision-maker. To be more precise, let $\bar{S}_i$ (resp. $\underline{S}_i$) be interest group i's gross payoff when the reform passes (resp. fails). Similarly, let $\bar{t}_i$ (resp. $\underline{t}_i$) represent the interest group's monetary contribution to the policy-maker in case the reform passes (resp. fails).

Two polar cases will be of a particular interest for what follows:

---

[6] For completeness, Appendix B develops an alternative model with a policy which is a continuous variable.

- *Congruent interest groups*: When $\bar{S}_i > \underline{S}_i$ for all $i \in \{1,..,n\}$, all principals find it worth to implement the reform. Passing the reform can thus be viewed as a public good to which all groups may want to contribute.
- *Conflicting interest groups*: When $\bar{S}_i > \underline{S}_i$ for $i \in \{1,..,k\}$ and $\bar{S}_i < \underline{S}_i$ for $i \in \{k+1,n\}$, the first k principals favor the reform, whereas the $n-k$ others are opposed to it. This corresponds to a fierce head-to-head competition between two opposite sets of interest groups.

It should be clear that we can normalize payoffs for each principal so that the worst political outcome from its own viewpoint yields zero payoff. In the case of groups who favor the reform, it boils down to adopting the normalization $\underline{S}_i = 0$, while $\bar{S}_i = 0$ prevails for groups that are opposed to this reform.[7]

The risk-neutral policy-maker has an opportunity cost $\psi(e)$ of increasing the probability that the reform is implemented. This disutility may stand for the cost of not allocating resources to private ends or, alternatively, the cost of not defending other causes in the policy arena. It is assumed that $\psi(e)$ is increasing, convex with a positive third derivative ($\psi' > 0, \psi'' > 0, \psi''' \geq 0$) and such that $\psi(0) = 0$. The Inada conditions $\psi'(0) = 0$ and $\psi'(1) = +\infty$ hold to insure interior solutions. Observe that the policy-maker has thus a bias toward the status quo since, in the absence of any influence, he would not exert any effort and the status quo would prevail.

The agent's expected payoff can thus be written as:

$$U = \mathbb{E}\left(\sum_{i=1}^n \tilde{t}_i \,\middle|\, e\right) - \psi(e). \tag{3.2}$$

For further references, we, respectively, denote by $\bar{T}_I = \sum_{i \in I} \bar{t}_i$ and $\underline{T}_I = \sum_{i \in I} \underline{t}_i$ the aggregate contribution of a coalition made of principals belonging to any subset $I \subseteq N$ while $\bar{T}_{-i}$ and $\underline{T}_{-i}$ denote the sum of the contributions of all principals except i in each state of nature. Similar notations are used throughout for the aggregate benefits $\bar{S}_I$ and $\underline{S}_I$ of such a coalition and for other variables of interest as well.

Timing: The lobbying game unfolds as follows.

1. Principals offer noncooperatively their state-contingent contribution schedules $\{(\bar{t}_i, \underline{t}_i)\}_{1 \leq i \leq n}$.

---

[7] This normalization has no impact on the net payoffs groups derive from the policy process, though it of course modifies their gross payoffs. It simplifies notations a lot, especially as far as proofs are concerned. Yet, intuitions are often better transmitted when using both payoffs, and we will often do so in the body of the Element.

2. The policy-maker decides which subset of contributions he should accept. If he refuses all such schedules, he obtains an exogenous payoff that is normalized at zero.
3. The policy-maker chooses the nonverifiable action e.
4. Finally, the political outcome, that is, whether the reform passes or fails, realizes. The payments stipulated by the contracts are made accordingly.

We are interested in studying the subgame-perfect equilibria of this *delegated common agency game* (Bernheim and Whinston, 1986b). The equilibrium set of bilateral relationships between the principals and the agent emerges endogenously at those equilibria.

Benchmarks. For further references, let us compute the socially optimal action e_N as

$$e_N = \arg\max_{e \in [0,1]} \mathbb{E}\left(\tilde{S}_N | e\right) - \psi(e).$$

The necessary and sufficient first-order condition for an interior optimum takes the form of a familiar Lindahl–Samuelson condition:

$$\overline{S}_N - \underline{S}_N = \psi'(e_N). \tag{3.3}$$

The marginal cost of effort is equal to the sum of the (algebric) marginal benefits.

As long as $\overline{S}_N > \underline{S}_N$, an assumption that is made throughout, e_N remains positive. When all interest groups have congruent preferences, this condition of course holds. More generally, it must be that principals in favor of the reform have a greater aggregate valuation for than principals against to get a positive effort, that is, $\sum_{i=1}^{k} \overline{S}_i > \sum_{i=k+1}^{n} \underline{S}_i$. When instead $\sum_{i=k+1}^{n} \underline{S}_i > \sum_{i=1}^{k} \overline{S}_i$, the optimal effort is at a corner, namely, $e_N = 0$. The socially optimal action is then to never implement the reform.

Consider now a coalition of principals $I \subset N$ and define as well the optimal action e_I for such a coalition as:

$$e_I = \arg\max_{e \in [0,1]} \mathbb{E}\left(\tilde{S}_I | e\right) - \psi(e).$$

Using a first-order condition yields

$$\overline{S}_I - \underline{S}_I = \psi'(e_I) \tag{3.4}$$

for an interior solution, while the corner solution $e_I = 0$ prevails if $\overline{S}_I < \underline{S}_I$.

For any subset of groups $I \subset N$, the aggregate payoff of the grand coalition made of the principals belonging to I together with the agent is defined as:

$$W_I = \mathbb{E}\left(\tilde{S}_I | e_I\right) - \psi(e_I). \tag{3.5}$$

Remark 1 Moral Hazard as the Source of Incompleteness in the "Social Contract." *Compared with the standard common agency model developed in Bernheim and Whinston (1986b), the specificity of our framework comes from the fact that the policy-maker's action e remains nonverifiable. This variable can be influenced by the different interest groups through the contributions they offer but it cannot be directly controlled and contracted upon. This assumption solves a basic tension in the common agency framework when applied to politics. If the agent's decision was contractible, as it is assumed in the political economy literature that built on common agency models under complete information, one could as well write a "social contract"[8] stipulating that the decision should maximize social welfare, where social welfare encompasses both the principals' and the agent's utility functions but also, maybe, the welfare of all groups which may have failed to organize. A simple forcing contract that would oblige the agent to implement the socially optimal action would suffice in fact. The fact that such a constitutional contract is institutionally feasible but a priori ruled out casts thus some doubts on the relevance of the standard common agency framework for a model of the political process. At best, there is a missing justification for the incompleteness of this "social contract."*

When the policy-maker's action is nonverifiable, as in our model, such constitutional contract based on actions can no longer be written. The question is whether a constitutional contract based on the contractible political outcomes could still be used and whether it would be interesting to use it. In this respect, note that even a benevolent Court of Law could not detect that the agent is not maximizing social welfare (at least in a one shot-relationship) given that all states are feasible with some probability under the full support assumption. Hence, it cannot be detected whether interest groups side-contract with the agent to change his decision. Constitutional contracts are of little help under moral hazard. This argument shows also that the natural framework to model the political process as a common agency game should make explicit the nonverifiability of the agent's action if one wants to justify the absence of any constitutional constraint on the agent's behavior.

4 Unrestricted Contracting

Suppose that there are no constraints whatsoever in the set of contracts that can be offered to the agent beyond satisfying his mere participation constraint.

---

[8] Of course, one could ask how this optimal social contract could emerge endogenously from the political game, especially if some groups fail to organize. But under the usual assumptions of the common agency framework, that is, complete information and transferable utility, there are good reasons to think that electoral competition should lead to such a contract.

We will coin this scenario as being one of *unrestricted contracting*. In contrast, Section 5 will investigate the case where some further constraints on payments arise.

4.1 Preliminaries

We start with a simple definition.

Definition 1 *An equilibrium of the delegated common agency game with a coalition A of active principals can be defined as a n-uple of contribution schedules* $\{(\bar{T}_i^D, \underline{T}_i^D)\}_{1 \leq i \leq n}$, *together with an effort level* e^D *such that:*

- *Given the contract offers, the policy-maker's expected utility cannot be greater by contracting with a different subset S ≠ A.*
- *The effort level* e^D *is optimally chosen by the decision-maker given the contribution schedules offered by the interest groups belonging to A.*
- *Each principal i's contract (both for active, i ∈ A and inactive, i ∉ A principals) is a best reply to what others have proposed given that the policy-maker's effort choice depends on the accepted contracts.*

It is slightly simpler for expositional purposes to start by writing down the conditions for a putative equilibrium where all principals would be active and have each their offer being accepted by the agent. We will then show in Appendix A that there cannot exist any other equilibrium with some principals not being active in the scenario of unrestricted contracting – that is, here under scrutiny.

Since all principals' offers are accepted at such an equilibrium, the following participation constraint of the agent has to be satisfied:

$$\max_{e \in [0,1]} \mathbb{E}\left(\bar{t}_i + \tilde{T}_{-i}^D | e\right) - \psi(e) \geq \max\left\{0, \mathbb{E}\left(\tilde{T}_S^D | e_S\right) - \psi(e_S)\right\}, \quad \text{for any } S \subset N.$$

$$(4.1)$$

The r.h.s of (4.1) describes what the agent can get by either refusing all offers or only accepting a subset of those offers. In particular, let e_S denote the optimal effort supply made by the agent when he accepts the aggregate contribution of principals in a coalition S. In fact, for an interior solution, the following first-order condition holds:

$$\bar{T}_S^D - \underline{T}_S^D = \psi'(e_S).$$

In turn, maximizing the l.h.s. of (4.1) immediately yields the following incentive constraint for an interior solution:

$$\bar{t}_i + \bar{T}_{-i}^D - \left(\underline{t}_i + \underline{T}_{-i}^D\right) = \psi'(e).$$

$$(4.2)$$

Consider now principal i's optimal offer when all other principals are active. It solves the following best-response problem:

$$(P_i^D): \qquad \max_{\{e,(\bar{t}_i,\underline{t}_i)\}} \mathbb{E}\left(\tilde{S}_i - \tilde{t}_i | e\right) \text{ subject to (4.1) and (4.2).}$$

Let us omit for the moment the incentive constraint (4.2). As it will be seen in Section 4.2, the equilibrium payments $(\bar{t}_i^D, \underline{t}_i^D)$ found will satisfy this constraint. Because principal i can decrease the expected payment to the common agent up to the point where the participation constraint (4.1) is binding, (P_i^D) can be written in a more compact way as:

$$\max_{e \in [0,1]} \left\{ \mathbb{E}\left(\tilde{S}_i + \tilde{T}_{-i}^D | e\right) - \psi(e) - \max\left\{0, \max_{S \subset N}\left(\mathbb{E}\left(\tilde{T}_S^D | e_S\right) - \psi(e_S)\right)\right\}\right\}.$$

The solution to this problem is to induce an effort e^D such that:

$$e^D \in \arg\max_{e \in [0,1]} \mathbb{E}\left(\tilde{S}_i + \tilde{T}_{-i}^D | e\right) - \psi(e). \tag{4.3}$$

This condition simply means that principal i does not want to induce another action than e^D given that the offers of all other principals are accepted. Each principal offers a contract which induces an action that maximizes the bilateral surplus of the coalition he forms with the common agent.

The following Lemma provides necessary and sufficient conditions for the $n+1$-uple $\left\{(\bar{t}_i^D, \underline{t}_i^D)_{1 \leq i \leq n}, e^D\right\}$ to be such an equilibrium where all principals are active.

Lemma 1 *The $n+1$-uple $\left\{(\bar{t}_i^D, \underline{t}_i^D)_{1 \leq i \leq n}, e^D\right\}$ is an equilibrium of the delegated common agency game where all principals are active if and only if:*

$$e^D \in \arg\max_{e \in [0,1]} \left\{\mathbb{E}\left(\tilde{T}_N^D | e\right) - \psi(e)\right\}, \tag{4.4}$$

$$e^D \in \arg\max_{e \in [0,1]} \left\{\mathbb{E}\left(\tilde{S}_i + \tilde{T}_{-i}^D | e\right) - \psi(e)\right\}, \qquad \textit{for all } i \in N, \tag{4.5}$$

$$\mathbb{E}\left(\tilde{S}_i + \tilde{T}_{-i}^D | e^D\right) - \psi(e^D) \geq \max_{\{i\} \subseteq S \subset N} \left\{\mathbb{E}\left(\tilde{S}_i + \tilde{T}_{S-\{i\}} | e_S\right) - \psi(e_S)\right\}, \tag{4.6}$$

$$\textit{for all } i \in N,$$

$$\mathbb{E}\left(\tilde{T}_N^D | e^D\right) - \psi(e^D) = \max_{S \subset N} \left\{0, \mathbb{E}\left(\tilde{T}_S^D | e_S\right) - \psi(e_S)\right\}. \tag{4.7}$$

This Lemma extends the analysis of Bernheim and Whinston (1986b) (complete information) and Laussel and Le Breton (1998a) (hidden information with ex ante contracting) to the case of moral hazard.

To build intuition behind conditions (4.4)–(4.7), note that (4.4) is simply the agent's incentive constraint when he faces an aggregate contribution $(\bar{T}_N, \underline{T}_N)$.

Condition (4.5) has been discussed above (see (4.3)). Condition (4.6) indicates that no principal finds it worth to make an offer that would bring the agent to exclude some principals. The grand-coalition forms. If condition (4.6) were not to hold for one principal, this principal could make an offer accepted by the agent who would contract then with only a subset of the principals.

Finally, condition (4.7) shows that the common agent should be indifferent between accepting the contracts of the grand-coalition N and accepting the next best option which is either to only accept contracts from a proper sub-coalition or to refuse all contracts at once. Indifference is definitively needed since, otherwise, one of the principals in the grand coalition could deviate, reduce payments in each state of nature $\bar{t}_i$ and $\underline{t}_i$ uniformly by the same small amount ε, while still inducing the same action e^D and acceptance of the whole range of contracts offered by the grand-coalition N.

4.2 Truthfulness and Efficiency

To characterize which (interior) efforts are equilibrium candidates, we use the necessary and sufficient first-order conditions for (4.4) and (4.5). This yields

$$\psi'(e^D) = \bar{T}_N^D - \underline{T}_N^D, \tag{4.8}$$

and

$$\psi'(e^D) = \bar{S}_i + \bar{T}_{-i}^D - \left(\underline{S}_i + \underline{T}_{-i}^D \right). \tag{4.9}$$

A common agency equilibrium with a nonnegative level of effort is thus such that:

$$\psi'(e^D) = \bar{T}_N^D - \underline{T}_N^D = \bar{S}_i + \bar{T}_{-i}^D - \left(\underline{S}_i + \underline{T}_{-i}^D \right). \tag{4.10}$$

From this, we deduce that the *marginal contribution* of each principal necessarily reflects his relative preferences among alternative political outcomes:

$$\bar{t}_i^D - \underline{t}_i^D = \bar{S}_i - \underline{S}_i, \tag{4.11}$$

or, with more compact notations,

$$\bar{t}_i^D = \tilde{S}_i - C_i^D, \tag{4.12}$$

where C_i^D is a fixed fee independent of the realization of the reform or not.

Equation (4.12) simply states that principal i's contribution is *truthful*. Payments perfectly reflect the benefits of the principal for each realized political outcome. Such a contribution schedule (4.12) thus aligns the objective of principal i with that of the common agent. Henceforth, even with moral hazard, the agent's incentive constraint is costless for the principals when contracts are unrestricted.

By offering a truthful schedule, a principal becomes indifferent at equilibrium among all realizations of the contractible outcomes. In our reform example, each principal can secure the same final payoff, namely C_i^D, whether the reform fails or succeeds. Determining the value of the principals' equilibrium payoff, and the sign of the transfers in each state of nature, is not yet possible at this stage. These issues are addressed in Section 4.3.

Since each principal offers a contribution which reflects his own relative valuation between alternative outcomes, the common agent ends up being *residual claimant* for the decision taken. He thus chooses the efficient level of effort from the point of view of the grand coalition he forms with all the principals. Indeed, using (4.8) and (4.12), an interior solution solves:

$$\psi'(e^D) = \overline{S}_N - \underline{S}_N. \tag{4.13}$$

Proposition 1 *In any equilibrium of the delegated common agency where all principals are active, the following properties hold:*

1. The efficient action is always implemented

$$e^D = e_N.$$

2. Equilibrium payments always satisfy the truthfulness criterion (4.12).

From standard moral hazard theory when applied to a single principal–agent relationship,[9] we already know that this principal obtains the first-best outcome by making the risk-neutral agent *residual claimant* for whatever decision he takes when this action is nonverifiable. This is obtained by using a truthful contribution of the form (4.12). Such contract makes the principal indifferent between all possible outcomes and has the agent pay a fixed fee C_i^D to the principal for the right of taking decisions. With multiple competing principals, the same result still holds. At a best response, each principal makes also the agent residual claimant and efficiency necessarily follows from the grand coalition's viewpoint.

Remark 2 Comparison with the Complete Information Scenario *Notice that the meaning of truthfulness in this moral hazard context should be somewhat distinguished from that given in Bernheim and Whinston (1986b). In Bernheim*

---

[9] See Laffont and Martimort (2002, ch. 4), for instance.

and Whinston (1986b), contributions can be conditioned on the agent's verifi-
able action and each principal using a truthful schedule is indifferent among
all the agent's actions. More precisely, these authors also show that there is no
loss of generality in restricting to non-negative contracts. The condition that
payments reflect the relative preferences over alternatives then only applies on
the positive range of those schedules. In a moral hazard framework, contrary
to Bernheim and Whinston (1986b)'s world of complete information, politi-
cal outcomes are not linked in a deterministic way to the common agent's
action. Nevertheless, because principals are indifferent among outcomes, their
expected payoffs is in fine independent of the agent's action. Even though
the contracting possibilities are not the same with and without moral hazard,
indifference among actions remains.

Remark 3 Truthfulness as an Equilibrium Property *It is also important to*
stress that, under moral hazard, truthfulness is no longer a restriction on the
equilibrium schedule which would lead to a refinement of the set of equilib-
rium outcomes as it is the case under complete information. The truthfulness
requirement is here endogenously obtained from looking at the first-order con-
ditions (4.9) and (4.10) for the agent and the principals, respectively. It is a
necessary feature of any best response. Under moral hazard and when a "full
support" assumption is satisfied by the stochastic mapping between actions and
outcomes, all contractible outcomes are feasible whatever the agent's action
(unless it is null). Hence, the issue of specifying the principals' contributions off
equilibrium disappears since all outcomes arise on the equilibrium path. This
is clearly a significant theoretical advantage of the moral hazard framework.
In equilibrium, contributions must be truthful.

4.3 Distribution of the Surplus

The only two remaining issues are to find whether such equilibria where all
principals are active exist and if yes what are the sets of fixed fees offered by
the principals. These fees determine the possible distributions of the aggregate
surplus among principals.

From the binding condition (4.7), which expresses the indifference of the
agent between contracting with the grand coalition and with the next best option
with a proper one, and the form of the equilibrium schedules, we deduce that
the vector $(C_i^D)_{1 \leq i \leq n}$ is a solution to the *fundamental equations:*

$$W_N - C_N^D = \max \left\{ 0, \max_{S \subset N} \left\{ W_S - C_S^D \right\} \right\}. \tag{4.14}$$

In a public good model with *hidden information and ex ante contracting*, Laussel and Le Breton (1998a) got a similar characterization of equilibrium payoffs by means of such equations. Our analysis borrows much from theirs.

Congruent Interest Groups. Here, we get:

Proposition 2 *The only equilibria of the delegated common agency game when principals have congruent preferences entail all principals being active. In any such equilibrium, principals get positive payoffs* $(C_i^D)_{1 \leq i \leq n}$ *and the common agent gets zero rent with:*

$$C_i^D \geq W_i > 0, \tag{4.15}$$

and

$$C_N^D = W_N. \tag{4.16}$$

With congruent preferences, the set of equilibrium payoffs of the delegated common agency game can be identified with the nonempty core of a cooperative game among principals having characteristic form $(W_S)_{S \subseteq N}$. Existence and properties immediately follow.

Two features of the equilibrium are worth noticing. First, when principals have congruent preferences, they all have in common the desire to extract the common agent's rent. Second, each of those principals has strong incentives to join the grand coalition of active principals to benefit from the increasing returns coming from the convexity of the cooperative game characterized with (3.5). Actually, the stand-alone payoffs W_i are payoffs obtained when each principal pays all the cost of the agent's effort. With congruent interests, this cost of effort, instead of being somehow duplicated for each principal when acting alone, is now jointly supplied by the coalition. Hence, there exists a surplus resulting from the joint contribution of multiple principals and the grand-coalition forms. This equilibrium aggregate surplus can be distributed in many different ways to give each principal more than the stand-alone payoff that he would get by being alone contracting with the decision-maker.

Conflicting Interest Groups. To simplify the analysis, we focus on the case of two principals who have opposite preferences on the benefit of the reform.

Proposition 3 *Assume that $n = 2$ and principals have conflicting preferences with principal 1 being dominant, that is, $\overline{S}_1 > \underline{S}_2$. Then, there exists a unique equilibrium of the delegated common agency game. In this equilibrium, the common agent gets a positive rent and both principals are active. Principal i gets a payoff:*

$$C_i^D = W_{12} - W_{-i} > 0. \tag{4.17}$$

The agent gets a residual payoff:

$$U = W_1 + W_2 - W_{12} > 0. \tag{4.18}$$

With conflicting preferences, the common agent can play one principal against the other and gets a positive rent out of this head-to-head competition. At the unique equilibrium of the game, each principal gets a payoff just equal to his incremental contribution to the aggregate coalition, as expressed in (4.17).

As noticed in Bernheim and Whinston (1986b) under complete information, this feature of the equilibrium under head-to-head competition is reminiscent of payments in a Groves mechanism although the comparison is somewhat misleading since the preferences of the competing principals are here common knowledge whereas, in the standard framework of Groves (1973), Clarke (1971), and Green and Laffont (1977), the preferences of contributing players are unknown to the mechanism designer.

Two common lessons can be withdrawn from Propositions 2 and 3. First, the equilibria of the delegated agency under moral hazard remain efficient, that is, there is neither free riding nor wasteful competition among principals. Second, all principals find it worth to intervene when they are unrestricted in the kind of contributions they may offer. This is the case whatever the nature of the competition between interest groups.

The agency problem that could arise under moral hazard between the common agent and his principals is not enough *alone* to explain why some groups may fail to operate in the policy arena. Under moral hazard, risk-neutrality, and *unrestricted contracting*, the political process efficiently aggregates the preferences of all principals and they are all active. If some groups are active in the lobbying process while others are not, the reasons must be found by modifying the lobbying model as it is; a route taken in Section 5.

Remark 4 Intrinsic versus Delegated Common Agency *As far as allocative efficiency is concerned, the delegated version of the common agency game and the intrinsic one, where the agent is constrained to accept all or none of the offered contracts, have the same efficient outcome. The two games differ only by their redistributive consequences because some further restrictions are put on the principals' payoffs under delegated common agency if (4.14) has to be satisfied. In Section 5 below, we will use the intrinsic common agency game to provide some intuition on the contractual externality that will emerge among principals. We will then show in Sections 6 and 7 that the two games differ in terms of their allocative and redistributive consequences when contributions are restricted and frictions in contracting appear.*

Remark 5 Intrinsic Preferences for Policy *For the sake of simplicity, we assume that the policy-maker has no intrinsic preference regarding the policy. This assumption is harmless when contracting is unrestricted. Assume that the agent gets a payoff $\overline{S}_0$ when the reform passes, and $\underline{S}_0$ otherwise. It is easy to see that (4.8) and (4.9) have to be modified by adding $\overline{S}_0 - \underline{S}_0$ on the r.h.s. This leaves (4.10) and (4.12) unchanged. In other words, principals design contracts that let the agent fully internalize his own intrinsic preferences with regard to the reform.*

Remark 6 More Complicated Patterns of Preferences Across Groups *The case $n > 2$ with the principals being either in favor or against the reform can be analyzed by merging the insights of Propositions 2 and 3. The characterization of the common agent's and the principals' payoffs is nevertheless not as clear as in the two polar cases described by those propositions.*

Remark 7 On Menus and Communication *Our assumption on the set of feasible contracts deserves further comments, especially in view of the literature on competitive equilibrium in insurance markets plagued with moral hazard (Pauly, 1974; Helpman and Laffont, 1975; Hellwig, 1983; Arnott and Stiglitz, 1991, among others). This literature has stressed the possible benefits of using so-called latent contracts. Those are contracts which are offered by a given principal but which are not used on path. Instead, those options would become attractive for the agent if the latter were contemplating a deviation from rival principals. In contrast, the contracts we consider are simple take-it-or-leave-it offers. The sole source of communication between the agent and any principal is the mere acceptance of the contract and there is no further round of communication beyond that stage.*

Let us a contrario suppose that each principal could commit to a whole menu of payments contingent on whether a reform takes place or not. Because of moral hazard, only those final outcomes are contractible and such menus exhaust all communication possibilities. In particular, those menus are not contingent on the offers made by other principals. Neither contracts on contracts (Peters and Szentes, 2012; Szentes, 2015) nor exclusivity requirements are allowed.[10] In this context, the agent accepts or refuses contracts and, in case of acceptance, simultaneously chooses from the menu offered by each principal at a further communication stage. It is straightforward that within his

---

[10] To motivate those assumptions, we notice that the contracts offered by other principals are nonobservable by a given principal which makes sense in a lobbying context where details of the arrangements between those principals and the agent are certainly kept private.

best-response correspondence, each principal has necessarily a take-it-or-leave-it offer. Henceforth, focusing on take-it-or-leave-it offer equilibria amounts to applying a refinement of the equilibrium set. This argument is very similar to that made by Berhneim and Whinston, (1986b) to justify a focus on truthful equilibria.

Some readers may dislike this argument, especially so because in our moral hazard context, this justification of truthfulness was not necessary. Indeed, it might be that some equilibrium outcomes can be reached with menus and communication that cannot be reached without. Certainly, moral hazard introduces so-called direct externalities across principals,[11] since effort depends on all contracts and the expected payoff of each principal thus directly depends on others' contracts. It is well known that such direct externalities are the source of a multiplicity of equilibria in menus.[12] Yet, we shall argue that most of those outcomes are unlikely in our context. First, notice that, once the agent is allowed to further communicate with a given principal by choosing within a nontrivial menu, consistency requires that we should also allow for further rounds of communication. To illustrate, a principal should be allowed to use these extra possibilities to secretly renegotiate with the agent. In particular, any state-contingent payment schedule that does not reach bilateral constrained efficiency (where constrained efficiency is required to account for the agent's moral hazard incentive constraint) should be renegotiated. Suppose this possibility for renegotiation is allowed. In our context with risk-neutral parties and no further constraints on transfers, the renegotiated offer is necessarily a truthful schedule. All such truthful schedules reflect the principal's payoff up to a constant. Hence, a menu of renegotiation-proof options is necessarily a menu of truthful schedules. But, the only such option that is taken both on and off-path by the agent is precisely the one that leaves the agent (resp. the principal) with the highest (resp. lowest) payoff. Hence, we are back to a scenario where the principal is only offering a trivial menu. When the game is de facto reduced to such take-it-or-leave-it offers, we get back to the characterization of equilibria given in Propositions 1, 2, and 3.

5 Nonnegative Payments: Preliminaries

The *truthful* schedules which emerge at equilibrium in the previous section are somewhat problematic because they entail negative transfers to the agent. Indeed, when a principal i favors the reform (resp. the status quo), the truthful schedule stipulates an equilibrium payment such that $\underline{t}_i = -C_i^D < 0 = \underline{S}_i$

---

[11] See Martimort (2007) for a taxonomy.

[12] Again we refer to Martimort and Stole (2003) and Martimort (2007), for examples.

(resp. $\bar{t}_i = -C_i^D < 0 = \bar{S}_i$). The agent is therefore willing to renege and refuse to pay back the group in case its most preferred outcome has not realized. To ensure that contracts are enforceable deals, it is thus natural to impose that all payments remain nonnegative.

This nonnegativity restriction has several key consequences. First, it renders the agency problem nontrivial; contributions no longer reflect preferences. Second, it endogenizes the set of active principals who offer positive contributions at equilibrium. Finally, it also generates inefficient outcomes for the political process. This approach thus allows us to ultimately link the redistributive and allocative aspects of the lobbying game, in sharp contrast with most of the existing lobbying literature relying on the common agency paradigm.

5.1 A Useful Lemma

Next Lemma simply states that groups that favor the reform do not pay when it is not passed, while it is the reverse for those groups hurt by the reform. This result significantly simplifies exposition.

Lemma 2 *There is no loss of generality in assuming that the agent accepts all contracts proposed when payments are nonnegative. Moreover, in any equilibrium, each principal offers a null contribution for an outcome that he does not favor:*

$$\tilde{S}_i = 0 \Rightarrow \tilde{t}_i = 0, \quad \forall i \in N.$$

Equipped with this result, we can now turn to the impact that various configurations of preferences and the types of behavior they involve have on equilibrium outcomes.

Imposing a nonnegativity constraint on payments simplifies the analysis of the acceptance stage of the game. Indeed, the agent is always (at least weakly) willing to accept any such contract. When principal i is *not active*, that is, proposes a null contribution for all outcomes, the agent is indifferent between accepting or rejecting his offer.

Remark 8 *It is worth noticing that the nonnegativity constraint on payments endogenously restricts strategies and equilibria to be "natural" as defined by Kirchsteiger and Prat (2001). One difference remains with the analysis of those authors. In their definition, contracts are contingent on actions, while in ours, they can only be contingent on outcomes as it becomes necessary in the present moral hazard context.*

5.2 The Cooperative Outcome

It it useful, both for getting a clue upfront for some of the frictions at play and for relevant comparisons, to start our analysis with the cooperative outcome. For future references, consider thus the hypothetical scenario where principals jointly design a nonnegative aggregate contribution. Possibly, this agreement may also stipulate ex ante lump sum payments to redistribute payoffs among principals. The policy-maker may either accept this joint offer or refuse all those offers at once.

The cooperative principals do not pay for their least-preferred outcome and thus

$$\underline{T}_N = 0. \tag{5.1}$$

The relevant nonnegativity constraint on aggregate payments thus boils down to

$$\bar{T}_N \geq 0. \tag{5.2}$$

Given an aggregate incentive scheme collectively offered by the n principals, the policy-maker thus chooses now an action e which solves:

$$\bar{T}_N = \psi'(e). \tag{5.3}$$

So doing yields to the common agent a payoff worth

$$U = e\bar{T}_N - \psi(e) = R(e), \tag{5.4}$$

where the *moral hazard rent*[13] $R(e) = e\psi'(e) - \psi(e)$ is nonnegative, increasing and convex with the assumptions made on $\psi(e)$ (namely, $R'(e) = e\psi''(e) > 0$, $R''(e) = e\psi'''(e) + \psi''(e) > 0$). From (5.4), it then follows that the agent's participation constraint necessarily holds. In other words, with nonnegative payments, the agent must necessarily be rewarded when the reform passes since he cannot be punished when it fails. He thus obtains a positive rent.

The cooperative outcome is then solution to the following problem:

$$(P^C): \qquad \max_{e \in [0,1]} \; e\left(\bar{S}_N - \underline{S}_N\right) - \psi(e) - R(e).$$

This expression showcases that the cooperative solution must balance efficiency considerations and the fact that inducing effort requires to leave a moral hazard rent $R(e)$ to the agent. This rent is costly from the cooperating principals' viewpoint. Of course, a similar trade-off arises in the noncooperative scenarios that will be investigated in Section 6.

---

[13] Laffont and Martimort (2002, ch. 4).

The solution to the cooperative problem (P^C) is straightforward. Because the reform is viewed as being valuable from the principals' grand-coalition viewpoint, namely $\bar{S}_N > \underline{S}_N$, the optimal effort e^C is interior and solves:

$$\bar{S}_N - \underline{S}_N = \psi'(e^C) + e^C \psi''(e^C). \tag{5.5}$$

This condition is again a familiar Lindahl–Samuelson condition for effort once it has been conveniently modified to account for the extra (marginal) cost of the agent's moral hazard rent $R'(e) = e\psi''(e)$.

To reduce the agent's moral hazard rent $R(e)$, the cooperating principals jointly reduce the aggregate payment made when the reform succeeds, namely, using (5.11):

$$\bar{T}^C = \bar{S}_N - \underline{S}_N - e^C \psi''(e^C). \tag{5.6}$$

As this condition shows, the existence of an agency cost $R(e)$ implies that, even when cooperating, principals as a whole shade their overall valuation for the reform. Because of such shading, their contribution is no longer truthful. We have

$$0 = \underline{T}^C < \bar{T}^C < \bar{S}_N - \underline{S}_N.$$

5.3 A Useful Benchmark: The Scenario of Intrinsic Common Agency

Consider now the hypothetical scenario where principals no longer cooperate in designing contracts but the game remains one of *intrinsic common agency*, an expression coined by Bernheim and Whinston (1986a). In this scenario, the agent has only two options. Either, he accepts all the principals' offers or none of those and thereby gets his reservation payoff which is normalized at zero. In this context, the only nonnegativity constraint on payments applies on the aggregate, namely:

$$\bar{t}_i + \bar{T}_{-i} = \bar{T}_N \geq 0 \tag{5.7}$$

while (5.1) still holds. Of course, the agent's rent in this context is still given by (5.4).

To give some intuition on the nature of the distortion, consider the case where all principals cooperate and share the agency cost needed to induce an effort e. Principal i then offers a contribution

$$\bar{t}_i^C = \bar{S}_i - \underline{S}_i - \frac{1}{n} e^C \psi''(e^C) \tag{5.8}$$

in case the reform passes which yields a payoff worth

$$V_i^C = \underline{S}_i + \frac{1}{n}(e^C)^2 \psi''(e^C). \tag{5.9}$$

Starting from such a cooperative contract, principal i, if he deviates by offering a lower transfer $\bar{t}_i$, induces another effort e_i which satisfies

$$\psi'(e_i) = \bar{t}_i + \overline{S}_{-i} - \underline{S}_{-i} - \frac{n-1}{n} e^C \psi''(e^C).\text{[14]}$$

Such a deviation thus yields an expected payoff to principal i which is worth:

$$V_i^d(e_i) = \underline{S}_i + e_i \left(\overline{S}_i - \underline{S}_i - \bar{t}_i\right) = \underline{S}_i + e_i \left(\overline{S}_N - \underline{S}_N - \frac{n-1}{n} e^C \psi''(e^C) - \psi'(e_i)\right).$$

It immediately follows that

$$\dot{V}_i^d(e^C) = -\frac{n-1}{n} e^C \psi''(e^C) < 0.$$

Hence, starting from the cooperative solution, principal i would like to induce a lower effort; an instance of negative externality among principals. By reducing his contribution and inducing a lower effort, principal i benefits from the fact that the remaining principals offer higher contributions while he also saves on the associated agency cost. This is the essence of the free-riding problem among noncooperating principals.

It turns out that the characterization of the equilibrium under intrinsic common agency already contains much information about what will happen under delegated common agency. In a first step toward such characterization, we observe that Lemma 2 and the fact that $\overline{S}_N > \underline{S}_N$ altogether imply that the aggregate incentive scheme offered by n principals satisfies

$$\underline{T}_N = \underline{t}_i + \underline{T}_{-i} = 0. \tag{5.10}$$

The policy-maker now chooses an action e which solves:

$$\psi'(e) = \overline{T}_N = \bar{t}_i + \overline{T}_{-i}. \tag{5.11}$$

So doing yields an expected payoff to the agent which is still given by (5.4).

Definition 2 *A vector $\left\{(\bar{t}_i^I, \underline{t}_i^I)_{i \le n}, e^I\right\}$ is an equilibrium of the intrinsic common agency game if and only if it solves for each principal i the following best-response optimization problem:*

$$(P_i^I): \quad \max_{\{\bar{t}_i, e\}} \mathbb{E}\left(\tilde{S}_i - \bar{t}_i | e\right) \text{ subject to (5.10) and (5.11).}$$

---

[14] For the purpose of our argument, it is enough to consider deviations which induce an effort level e_i which is interior.

Inserting (5.10) into the above maximand and using the incentive constraint (5.11), we rewrite this program in terms of a sole maximization with respect to the effort level that principal i can induce as

$$(P_i^J)' : \quad \max_{e \in [0,1]} e \left(\overline{S}_i - \underline{S}_i + \overline{T}_{-i}^J - \underline{T}_{-i}^J \right) - \psi(e) - R(e).$$

The intrinsic common agency game is known to be an *aggregate game* at least since Bernheim and Whinston (1986a). In such a game, the payoff of each principal depends on his own payments and those of others only through the overall aggregate payment that induces a given effort level. Sometimes, those games are known to have nice properties in the sense that their equilibria can be found as solution to a *self-generating problem* as we will soon see below. This is the *Principle of Aggregate Concurrence* as coined by Martimort and Stole (2012). This reduction captures the fact that, in such an aggregate game, the objectives of the different principals can be somehow aligned. Intuitively, because the non-negativity and the agent's incentive constraints depend only on the aggregate payment, any given principal, since he is unrestricted in his own payment, can always undo whatever payments are offered by others without changing the feasibility set. This creates a common concern across principals and aligns their objectives.

To see how, observe that if the equilibrium effort e^J is a solution for all problems $(P_i^J)'$, it is also a solution for the sum of those optimization problems, namely, for the so-called *self-generating* optimization problem:

$$(P^{SE}) : \quad \max_{e \in [0,1]} e \left(\overline{S}_N - \underline{S}_N + (n-1)(\overline{T}^J - \underline{T}^J) \right) - n\psi(e) - nR(e),$$

where $\underline{T}^J = 0$ from (5.10) and the equilibrium level of effort satisfies

$$\psi'(e^J) = \overline{T}^J. \tag{5.12}$$

This problem is *self-generating* because its solution e^J is also an argument of the maximand.

It should be clear from the nonnegativity constraint (5.10) that there exists a continuum of possible equilibria of the intrinsic common agency game that are defined up to a redistribution of payments across principals even though the equilibrium effort remains the same across such equilibria. For the sake of comparison with the delegated common agency scenario where this constraint is taken principal by principal, we shall concentrate on one such redistribution where

$$\underline{t}_i^J = 0 \quad \forall i. \tag{5.13}$$

We summarize the result of this optimization and the main features of this equilibrium in the next proposition.

Proposition 4 *There exists a unique equilibrium of the intrinsic common agency game such that (5.13) holds. The following properties hold.*

1. *Effort is below the cooperative outcome;*

$$e^I < e^C$$

with e^I that solves

$$\overline{S}_N - \underline{S}_N = \psi'(e^I) + ne^I\psi''(e^I). \tag{5.14}$$

2. *Principal i offers contributions:*

$$\overline{t}_i^I = \overline{S}_i - \underline{S}_i - e^I\psi''(e^I) \text{ and } \underline{t}_i^I = 0 \quad \forall i. \tag{5.15}$$

In the intrinsic common agency game, each principal takes as given the contributions of others when choosing how much to pay himself for the agent's services. Inducing a higher level of effort from the agent becomes a public good as it can be easily seen from the agent's incentive constraint (5.11). In equilibrium, underprovision of this public good follows from the principals' noncooperative behavior. The equilibrium effort is lower than if principals were jointly designing the agent's contribution. Indeed, all principals care about extracting the agent's moral hazard rent $R(e)$ and, doing so, they induce a lower level of effort than at the first best. From (5.15), everything happens as if each principal had to pay exactly for the marginal agency cost of this rent, namely: $R'(e) = e\psi''(e)$. As a result of this compounding of rent extraction across principals, there is now a *n*-fold distortion of the effort level below the first best. The equilibrium effort level under intrinsic common agency is thus lower than if principals had cooperated and internalized the free-riding externality.

It should be clear from our analysis that the free-riding problem under intrinsic common agency comes from the fact that the agent withdraws some positive rent when aggregate payments are constrained to be nonnegative and, because actions are nonverifiable, this rent is linked to his effort level. It is in sharp contrast with the case of unrestricted contracting. There, the agent can still withdraw some positive rent; the case of conflicting interests analyzed in Section 4.3 is an example in order. Yet, this rent only depends on how principals compete to get a share of the overall surplus. With unrestricted contracting, redistributive and allocative issues are disentangled and the agent's effort is set at the first best independently on how the surplus is shared among principals. Because the agent always exerts the first-best effort, no free riding arises.

6 Nonnegative Payments and Delegated Agency: Congruent Interests

Consider now the scenario of delegated common agency. The main conceptual difficulty here is that the common agency game, although it remains an *aggregate game*, fails to satisfy the *Principle of Aggregate Concurrence*. Because each principal is now restricted to offering a nonnegative payment, he cannot *always* undo whatever aggregate payment is offered by others. Even worse, this constraint may push this principal out of the influence process.

To see how, we start with the case where the n principals have all congruent preferences and favor the reform. Remember that, in this setting, we have made the normalization $\underline{S}_i = 0$, which is without loss of generality.

Given any aggregate incentive scheme, the effort e still solves (5.11), and the common agent gets an information rent which is again given by (5.4).

Remember that a group that favors the reform never pays when it fails, that is, $\underline{t}_i = 0$ for all $i \in N$. The nonnegativity condition on payments, which is now taken principal by principal, then boils down to

$$\bar{t}_i \geq 0 \quad \text{for all } i \in N. \tag{6.1}$$

This constraint together with the incentive constraint (5.11) implies that principal i can only implement any effort e that satisfies

$$\psi'(e) \geq \bar{T}_{-i}. \tag{6.2}$$

In other words, principal i can increase effort with respect to what other principals would do in his absence but he can never reduce it.

Definition 3 *A* $n + 1$*-uple* $\left\{ (\bar{t}_i^D, \underline{t}_i^D)_{i \leq n}, e^D \right\}$ *is an equilibrium of the delegated common agency game with congruent principals if and only if* $\underline{t}_i^D = 0$ *and it solves for each principal i the following best-response optimization problem:*

$$(P_i^D): \quad \max_{\{\bar{t}_i, e\}} e\left(\bar{S}_i - \bar{t}_i\right) \text{ subject to (5.11) and (6.1).}$$

Inserting (6.1) into the maximand and the incentive constraint (5.11), we rewrite this program in terms of a sole maximization with respect to the effort level that principal i can induce as

$$(P_i^D): \quad \max_{e \in [0,1]} e\left(\bar{S}_i + \bar{T}_{-i}\right) - \psi(e) - R(e) \text{ subject to (6.2).}$$

When (6.2) is binding at the best response for principal i, his contribution is zero and this principal is de facto not active. Equilibria where the grand coalition of principals emerges but where some principals make no contribution can be identified with equilibria where only a proper coalition of those principals emerges. Indeed, the presence of the new constraint (6.2) shows that the set of principals who offer a positive contribution may be a proper subset of N. Then, the action chosen by the policy-maker no longer maximizes the aggregate pay-off of the grand coalition made of all principals subject to the agent's incentive constraint but that of this proper sub-coalition.

It is important to stress that, with nonnegative payments, the distribution of the surplus between the principals and the agent is linked to the level of effort which emerges in equilibrium. When constraint (6.2) binds, the effort level depends on the preferences of the only active principals; those who offer positive contributions.

6.1 Contributions and Allocative Inefficiency

To better understand the structure of the equilibrium, we now rank the different principals according to their increasing valuations for the reform in such a way that $\bar{S}_1 < \bar{S}_2 \cdots < \bar{S}_n$. To simplify presentation, we assume for the time being that all principals have different preferences. A straightforward extension would consist in allowing for different principals with the same preferences, an exercice that we will undertake later.

The allocative properties of the equilibrium are investigated in the next proposition.

Proposition 5 *Assume that all principals have congruent preferences; then there exists a unique equilibrium of the delegated common agency game. The following properties hold.*

1. The equilibrium effort is $e^D = e_k$, where

$$\sum_{i=n-k+1}^{n} \bar{S}_i = \psi'(e_k) + k e_k \psi''(e_k). \tag{6.3}$$

2. The number k of active principals who offer a positive contribution in equilibrium is defined as

$$n - k + 1 = \min_i \left\{ i | \bar{S}_i - e_i \psi''(e_i) \geq 0 \right\}. \tag{6.4}$$

3. Contributions are given by

$$\bar{t}_i^D = \max\{\bar{S}_i - e_k \psi''(e_k), 0\}. \tag{6.5}$$

6.1.1 Active Set of Principals

To understand this equilibrium characterization, it is useful to start with what we already know from the equilibrium characterization under intrinsic common agency. From (5.15) and taking into account our assumption that $\underline{S}_i = 0$ for principals who favor the reform, we observe that payments in any intrinsic common agency equilibrium are given as

$$\bar{t}_i^I = \bar{S}_i - e^I \psi''(e^I).$$

Clearly, those payments cannot be part of an equilibrium under delegated agency if $\bar{S}_i$ is small enough since it would violate the nonnegativity constraint (6.1). Those principals with the lowest valuations, that is, valuations which stand below the marginal agency cost $R'(e^I) = e^I \psi''(e^I)$, are pushed out of the political process. Under delegated agency, those principals being out, the magnitude of the free-riding problem diminishes among the remaining active principals. As a result the agent's effort increases, which means that the (marginal) agency cost also increases and might push out of the process even principals with higher valuation. Because principals are ranked according to their increasing valuations for the reform, that subset of active principals is an upper tail of the distribution of principals. Equation (6.4) defines then the endogenous cut-off on valuations above which principals become active contributors. The size k of the active coalition is precisely found when the bringing in of an extra principal with a "marginal valuation" just covers the marginal agency cost at the effort level that such coalition would induce. More formally, adding a $k + 1$th inframarginal principal with valuation $\bar{S}_{n-k}$ only increases the effort level if and only if

$$\bar{S}_{n-k} > e_{k+1} \psi''(e_{k+1}).$$

6.1.2 Virtual Valuations

Under moral hazard and with the added constraint of having nonnegative contributions, everything happens as under complete information except that the valuation of each principal $\bar{S}_i$ is now replaced by a *virtual valuation* which is effort-dependent, namely

$$\tilde{S}_i(e) \equiv \max\{0, \bar{S}_i - e\psi''(e)\}.$$

This virtual valuation now takes into account the marginal cost of the agent's rent which is borne by this principal. Since this cost is the same for all principals, some of them, the weakest ones, fail to intervene.

This remark been made, it becomes useful to rewrite the equilibrium condition in a more compact way as the solution to the following Lindahl–Samuelson condition conveniently modified to account for informational frictions:

$$\sum_{i=1}^{n} \max\left\{0, \bar{S}_i - e^D \psi''(e^D)\right\} = \psi'(e^D). \tag{6.6}$$

This more compact expression first stresses the nature of the exact contribution of each principal. Second, it implicitly encompasses also the determination of the set of active principals. Lastly, it easily generalizes the previous approach to the case where principals may have the same preferences, a scenario that is covered in Corollary 1 below.

6.1.3 Free Riding

Formula (6.6) shows that free riding among interest groups actually takes two different forms. First, active principals reduce their contributions below their incremental benefits of the reform to account for the rent they leave to the agent. For those principals free riding is at the *intensive margin*. Second, some principals remain out of the political process. Free riding takes place at the *extensive margin* for those principals. This novel aspect is key to understand that the grand coalition of principals may fail to be active in sharp contrast with the scenario of intrinsic agency or the scenario with unrestricted contracting.

6.1.4 Homogenous Principals

Consider the case where all principals are alike and have congruent preferences in favor of the reform.

Corollary 1 *Assume that all principals gets a fixed benefit from the reform, that is,* $\bar{S}_i = \bar{S} > 0$ *for any* $i \in \{1, \ldots, n\}$.

1. The equilibrium effort level entails a n-fold distortion:

$$n\bar{S} = \psi'(e^D) + ne^D\psi''(e^D). \tag{6.7}$$

2. All principals are active in equilibrium:

$$\bar{t}_n = \bar{S} - e^D\psi''(e^D) = \frac{\psi'(e^D)}{n} > 0. \tag{6.8}$$

When n increases, two effects are at play. First, when the per capita benefit $\bar{S}$ of the reform remains unchanged, the overall benefits of the reform that accrue to the group grows linearly with n. Second, as the size of the group increases, the free-riding problem also gets worse. It turns out that, as a result of those two countervailing forces, the equilibrium effort e^D increases as it can be readily seen from (6.7). Such congruent principals actually display all features of what Olson (1965) coined as being an *inclusive group*. An inclusive group has its members willing to accept newcomers and, in this case, the supply of the collective good increases with the size of the group.

As n goes large, each individual contribution should have little impact on the probability of a reform. Minimizing his own contribution is then the sole objective of any given principal. When evaluating whether to contribute or not, this individual thus compares his benefit $\bar{S}$ with the marginal agency cost at the (limiting) equilibrium effort e_∞. This effort is determined by the indifference condition:[15]

$$\lim_{n \to +\infty} \bar{t}_n = 0 \Leftrightarrow \bar{S} = e_\infty \psi''(e_\infty).$$

Although each individual contribution becomes arbitrarily small as the size of the group goes out of bound, the probability of the reform nevertheless remains bounded away from zero.

Consider instead the alternative scenario where the per capita benefit of the reform writes as $\bar{S}(n) = \frac{\Sigma}{n}$; in other words, each principal now gets an equal share of a fixed-size benefit of the reform. It is straightforward to adapt our previous reasoning to get that, in the limit, while $\lim_{n \to +\infty} \bar{t}_n = 0$, we have also $e_\infty = 0$. In other words, there is now a strong form of free riding with no reform being implemented in the limit.

This discussion is reminiscent of some earlier findings in the mechanism design literature. There, free riding might arise due to private information on the valuations of agents who voluntarily participate to a mechanism for the provision of a public good. Whether the free-riding problem holds or not in the limit of a large economy depends on the comparison between the per capita cost of provision and the sum of the individuals' information rent. In this respect, Mailath and Postlewaite (1990) and Hellwig (2003) reach different conclusions on the magnitude of the free-riding problem in the limit of a large economy when making different assumptions on how this per capita cost varies with the size of the population.

6.1.5 Heterogenous Principals

The striking lesson of Proposition 5 and Corollary 1 is that heterogeneity among the principals is a key factor to explain the failure of some of them to intervene and contribute. The virtual valuation of the weakest principals may be zero, and those principals end up having no influence on the political process.

---

[15] Assumptions about ψ guarantee that the solution to $\bar{S} = e_\infty \psi''(e_\infty)$ lies in $(0, 1)$, which is enough for the result.

Example 1 *Denote* $n = n_1 + n_2$ *where* n_i *is the number of principals having valuations* $\bar{S}_i$ *(i* = 1, 2), *with* $\bar{S}_1 < \bar{S}_2$. *Suppose also that* $\psi(e) = \frac{e^2}{2\mu}$ *for some positive parameter* μ *small enough.*[16] *From (6.6), the effort level is given by*

$$e_k = \mu\frac{(k - n_2)\bar{S}_1 + n_2\bar{S}_2}{1 + k}$$

if the number of active principals $k \geq n_2$ *is such that* $e_{k+1} > \mu\bar{S}_1 > e_k$. *This gives:*

$$k = \begin{cases} n \ if & \bar{S}_2 > \bar{S}_1 \geq \frac{n_2}{n_2+1}\bar{S}_2, \\ n_2 \ if & \frac{n_2}{n_2+1}\bar{S}_2 > \bar{S}_1. \end{cases} \qquad (6.9)$$

When the preferences of the two interest groups are sufficiently far apart, only those principals who value the good the most contribute. Instead, when there is less heterogeneity among groups, all principals find it worth to intervene. This result offers a striking illustration of Olson (1965)'s well-known *exploitation of the great by the small*. Interestingly, condition (6.9) that determines whether principals with a lower valuation will participate to the political process depends on n_2 alone. When considering to become active, a principal with valuation $\bar{S}_1$ will only compare the cost of increasing the agent's effort with his own benefit from the decision. As n_2 increases, the free-riding problem will become more and more severe, up to the point where all principals with a lower valuation remain inactive, even though the aggregate value for them, as a group, of an increase of the effort by the agent may become arbitrarily large.

As discussed in the introduction, this result is driven by the fact that the aggregate value of the decision increases for active principals. If we make n_2 vary while keeping $n_2\bar{S}_2 \equiv \bar{\Sigma}_2$ constant, principals from the first group will remain inactive when $\bar{S}_1 < \frac{1}{1+n_2}\bar{\Sigma}_2$. This condition becomes more stringent when n_2 increases. As free riding gets stronger among high valuation principals, it becomes more difficult to rely only on their contributions, and principals with a lower valuation are more likely to enter the game of influence.

Using $\bar{\Sigma}_2$ as the measure of the aggregate valuation of the reform for high valuation principals, and n_2 as a measure of the size of this group ceteris paribus, in order to better separate the different effects, we can summarize this discussion:

Corollary 2 *An interest group with a low valuation is less likely to contribute when it faces another group with a higher aggregate valuation,* $\bar{\Sigma}_2$, *and a smaller size,* n_2.

---

[16] Although the Inada conditions are not satisfied by this disutility function, we shall focus on constellation parameters where solutions remain interior so that our analysis carries over.

Putting Corollaries 1 and 2 altogether suggests that the form that free riding among interest groups takes, that is whether it is by means of weak contributions or even no participation at all, indeed depends on the surrounding environment and the force that existing competing groups exert also on the political process. It is not enough to specify exogenously a pressure function which depends on group size as Becker (1983, 1985) repeatedly did. This function should also depend on the composition of other groups as well.[17]

Redistributing benefits across contributors making them more symmetric while keeping the total benefit constant might thus have a nonneutral impact on whether the reform is implemented or not. Indeed, political participation by more principals is more likely as those principals are more symmetric. However, as more principals get involved, free riding is also exacerbated and the probability of a reform decreases. This tension is illustrated in the following example.

Example 2 *Take $n = 2$ and suppose also that, as before, $\psi(e) = \frac{e^2}{2\mu}$. Consider first a setting with principal 1 having valuation $\overline{S}$ and principal 2 having zero valuation for the reform. The equilibrium level of effort is such that*

$$e^D = \frac{\mu \overline{S}}{2}.$$

Consider now a redistribution of the benefits of the reform toward a symmetric setting where both principals get $\frac{\overline{S}}{2}$ out of the reform. The equilibrium level of effort is now such that

$$e^D = \frac{\mu \overline{S}}{3}.$$

The redistribution, although it increases political participation since now both principals intervene, decreases the likelihood of the reform. These results are in line with the Olson-Stigler's proposition that states that collective action will be more successful as benefits are more heterogeneous among actors with congruent preferences.

This result should of course be contrasted with the well-known *Neutrality Theorem* in the public economics literature. This theorem establishes that the

---

[17] This point echoes some findings we made elsewhere in Lefebvre and Martimort (2020). There, we append to the model of lobbying competition à la Grossman and Helpman (1994) a group formation stage where individuals, privately informed on their valuations for the policy on sale, design a revelation mechanism to first share the cost of influence and second choose what sort of influence to exert on the policy-maker. The informational asymmetry frictions that preclude efficiency within the group are determined, at equilibrium, by the force that other groups exert on the political process and those forces depend themselves in turn on their own frictions.

voluntary provision of public good is independent of the wealth distribution among contributors – a result found in Warr (1983), Bergstrom, Blume, and Varian (1986), and Bernheim (1986) among others. The second of these papers nevertheless argues that the neutrality result holds only if the set of contributors does not change as a result of the wealth redistribution among contributors. This is precisely a similar failure of neutrality which may happen here as well when some groups fail to intervene because of the moral hazard frictions.[18]

6.2 Distribution of the Equilibrium Surplus

We conclude this section with some results on the distribution of the equilibrium surplus.

Proposition 6 *Assume that all principals have congruent preferences.*

1. All active principals making positive contributions get the same equilibrium payoff:

$$C_i^D = e_k^2 \psi''(e_k) \qquad for \ i \in \{n - k + 1, \ldots, n\}, \tag{6.10}$$

where k is defined as in (6.4) and e_k is the equilibrium effort given by (6.3).
2. Equilibrium payoffs of the inactive principals depend on their valuations:

$$C_i^D = e_k \bar{S}_i \qquad for \ i \in \{1, \ldots, n - k\}. \tag{6.11}$$

The fact that active principals all get the same payoffs is already an important feature of the intrinsic common agency scenario.[19] It carries over to delegated common agency. This feature captures the fact that those active principals end up having aligned objectives. In other words, the *Principle of Aggregate Concurrence* applies for this subset. For those active principals, any ex ante redistribution of the benefits of the reform by means of lump-sum payments has also no impact on their equilibrium payoff. This payoff only depends on the equilibrium effort and this variable remains unchanged through such redistribution. Instead, the equilibrium payoffs of inactive principals depend on their valuation and such ex ante redistribution makes winners and losers.

---

[18] Interestingly, replacing "wealth" by "benefits of the reform," the results of Theorem 4 in Bergstrom, Blume, and Varian (1986), that link redistribution among players, set of contributors and production of public good, hold unchanged in our context.

[19] Remember that $\underline{S}_i = 0$ for those groups.

7 Nonnegative Payments and Delegated Agency: Conflicting Interests

Let us now turn to the case of two interest groups having conflicting interests. Principal 1 is pro reform, whereas principal 2 opposes it.

From Lemma 2, we can restrict the analysis to the case where principal 1 (resp. principal 2) offers a nonnegative contribution $\bar{t}_1$ (resp. $\underline{t}_2$) when the reform succeeds (resp. when it fails) with the further requirement $\underline{t}_1 = 0$ (resp. $\bar{t}_2 = 0$). The agent's incentive constraint can now be written as

$$\psi'(e) = \bar{t}_1 - \underline{t}_2, \tag{7.1}$$

with his payoff being now expressed as

$$\underline{t}_2 + R(e). \tag{7.2}$$

Two remarks are worth making. First, the agent's effort supply is now increasing with the difference in the contributions of both principals. This incentive constraint captures the extend to which principals with opposite preferences compete to increase or reduce the probability of adopting the reform.

Second, and in comparison with the case of congruent principals, the agent now benefits from the contribution of the group opposed to the reform to raise his payoff. To induce acceptance by the agent of his own offer, principal 1 must thus offer a contribution which satisfies

$$\underline{t}_2 + R(e) \geq \max_{e \in [0,1]} \left\{ (1 - e)\underline{t}_2 - \psi(e) \right\}.$$

When, as requested by the nonnegativity constraint,

$$\underline{t}_2 \geq 0, \tag{7.3}$$

the r.h.s. is maximized at $e = 0$. The agent's participation constraint thus becomes

$$R(e) \geq 0,$$

which obviously holds for any nonnegative effort level, that is, when principal 1's contribution exceeds that of principal 2:

$$\bar{t}_1 \geq \underline{t}_2.^{20} \tag{7.4}$$

---

[20] Principal 1 will choose such a contribution, instead of remaining inactive, in which case the agent exerts zero effort and the reform never arises, if

$$e(\bar{S}_1 - \bar{t}_1) \geq \underline{S}_1 = 0.$$

We will omit this constraint, and check ex post that it is satisfied.

Definition 4 *A triplet* $\left\{\bar{t}_1^D, \underline{t}_2^D, e^D\right\}$ *is an equilibrium of the delegated common agency game with conflicting principals if and only if* $\underline{t}_1^D = \bar{t}_2^D = 0$ *and it solves the following best-response optimization problems for principal 1 and 2, respectively:*

$$(P_1^D): \qquad \max_{\{\bar{t}_1, e\}} \mathbb{E}\left(\bar{S}_1 - \bar{t}_1\right) \text{ subject to (7.1) and (7.4)}$$

and

$$(P_2^D): \qquad \max_{\{e, t_2\}} (1 - e)(\underline{S}_2 - \underline{t}_2) \text{ subject to (7.1) and (7.3)}.$$

We are now ready to state our main result in this section.

Proposition 7 *Assume that principals have conflicting preferences with* $\bar{S}_1 > \underline{S}_2$ *and that* $(1 - e)\psi'(e)$ *is concave in* e.[21] *Then, there exists an unique equilibrium of the delegated common agency game with a positive effort level* e^D *given by:*

$$\bar{S}_1 - e^D \psi''(e^D) = \max\left\{\underline{S}_2 - (1 - e^D)\psi''(e^D), 0\right\} + \psi'(e^D). \tag{7.5}$$

Again, a principal is active if his valuation for or against the reform exceeds the marginal agency cost he pays to the agent. With conflicting preferences, however, the two principals differ with respect to those agency costs since they pay for the agent's services in different states of nature.

Expressed in terms of their virtual marginal valuations, we thus have, for the pro-reform principal

$$\tilde{\bar{S}}_1(e) = \max\{\bar{S}_1 - e\psi''(e), 0\},$$

while for the against-reform principal, we instead have

$$\tilde{\underline{S}}_2(e) = \max\{\underline{S}_2 - (1 - e)\psi''(e), 0\}.$$

The equilibrium condition (7.5) just says that the modified Lindahl–Samuelson condition now takes a familiar expression that reflects the relative weights of the two groups when informational frictions matter:

$$\tilde{\bar{S}}_1(e^D) - \tilde{\underline{S}}_2(e^D) = \psi'(e^D).$$

---

[21] This property ensures concavity of principal 2's problem (P_2), that is, $(1 - e)\psi'''(e) < 2\psi''(e)$, a condition which necessarily holds when e is close enough to one.

Example 3 *Consider again the case where $\psi(e) = \frac{e^2}{2\mu}$ for μ small enough. The equilibrium condition (7.5) becomes*

$$
e^D = \begin{cases} \mu \frac{(\frac{1}{\mu} + \bar{S}_1 - \underline{S}_2)}{3} & \text{if } \bar{S}_1 > 2(\frac{1}{\mu} - \underline{S}_2) \\ \mu \frac{\bar{S}_1}{2} & \text{if } \bar{S}_1 \leq 2(\frac{1}{\mu} - \underline{S}_2). \end{cases} \tag{7.6}
$$

Example 3 shows that principal 2 does not contribute when $\underline{S}_2$ is sufficiently small with respect to $\bar{S}_1$. In that case, the principal who favors the reform is the only one who can pay for the marginal agency cost necessary to influence the agent.

When both groups intervene at equilibrium, the countervailing power of principal 2 acts like a brake to the reform. The probability of success is lower than if only group 1 intervenes since $\frac{\frac{1}{\mu} + \bar{S}_1 - \underline{S}_2}{3} < \frac{\bar{S}_1}{2}$ when $\bar{S}_1 < 2(\frac{1}{\mu} - \underline{S}_2)$.[22]

Example 4 *Consider now the case of three different kinds of principals having different preferences. More precisely, n_1 principals favor the reform and have valuation $\bar{S}_1$; n_2 other principals also favor the reform but have a greater valuation $\bar{S}_2 > \bar{S}_1$; whereas n_3 principals prefer the status quo and have valuation $\underline{S}_3$. Generalizing (7.5), it is straightforward to verify that the equilibrium effort solves:*

$$
n_1 \max \left\{ 0, \bar{S}_1 - e^D \psi''(e^D) \right\} + n_2 \left(\bar{S}_2 - e^D \psi''(e^D) \right) = \psi'(e^D)
$$
$$
+ n_3 \max \left\{ \underline{S}_3 - (1 - e^D) \psi''(e^D), 0 \right\}. \tag{7.7}
$$

Still using the quadratic specification $\psi(e) = \frac{e^2}{2\mu}$, an equilibrium with all principals being active yields an effort level e^D given by:

$$
e^D = \mu \frac{n_1 \bar{S}_1 + n_2 \bar{S}_2 + n_3 (\frac{1}{\mu} - \underline{S}_3)}{1 + n_1 + n_2 + n_3} \quad \text{if} \quad \bar{S}_1 > \frac{n_2 \bar{S}_2 + n_3 (\frac{1}{\mu} - \underline{S}_3)}{1 + n_2 + n_3}
$$
$$
\text{and} \quad \underline{S}_3 > \frac{n_1 + n_2 + 1 - \mu n_1 \bar{S}_1 - \mu n_2 \bar{S}_2}{\mu (1 + n_1 + n_2)}.
$$

---

[22] The comparison with the case of unrestricted contracting is not immediate, since frictions reduce both groups' ability to influence the decision. It is interesting to note that while the apparition of frictions unambiguously tilts the policy toward making the reform more likely when $\bar{S}_1 > 2(\frac{1}{\mu} - \underline{S}_2)$, results are more contrasted with lower values of $\bar{S}_1$, and that although principal 2 now does not contribute. More precisely, the apparition of frictions increases the probability of the reform if $2\underline{S}_2 < \bar{S}_1 < 2(\frac{1}{\mu} - \underline{S}_2)$.

The condition on $\overline{S}_1$ is more stringent than $\overline{S}_1 > \frac{n_2}{1+n_2}\overline{S}_2$ if and only if [23]

$$\frac{n_1 + n_2 + 1 - \mu n_1\overline{S}_1 - \mu n_2\overline{S}_2}{\mu(1 + n_1 + n_2)} < \underline{S}_3 < \frac{1 + n_2 - \mu n_2\overline{S}_2}{\mu(1 + n_2)}.$$

Type 1 principals intervene less often in the presence of type 3 principals than in their absence. The countervailing power of group 3 impacts at two levels. Not only those principals directly influence the policy-maker to reduce the likelihood of a reform but the mere presence of this group also makes it harder for type 2 principals with mild preferences to intervene.

Again, Example 4 points at the fact that whether an interest group intervenes or not in the political arena depends on the landscape of competing groups, their objectives and their ability to influence the whole political process.

Remark 9 Intrinsic Preferences (Redux) *When the policy-maker has some intrinsic preferences over the outcome, it is easy to see that the modified Lindahl–Samuelson (6.6) with congruent groups has to be amended into*

$$\sum_{i=1}^{n} \max\left\{0, \overline{S}_i - e^D\psi''(e^D)\right\} + \overline{S}_0 - \underline{S}_0 = \psi'(e^D),$$

where we keep $\overline{S}_0 - \underline{S}_0$ small enough in absolute values to keep an interior solution $e^D \in (0, 1)$. It immediately follows that having a policy-maker biased in favor of the reform ($\overline{S}_0 > \underline{S}_0$) leads to higher provision of the effort, associated to more free riding at the extensive margin. The reverse holds with a policy-maker who is biased against the reform.

With conflicting groups, the Lindahl–Samuelson condition (7.5) becomes

$$\max\left\{\overline{S}_1 - e^D\psi''(e^D), 0\right\} + \overline{S}_0 - \underline{S}_0 = \max\left\{\underline{S}_2 - (1 - e^D)\psi''(e^D), 0\right\} + \psi'(e^D).$$

Again, a pro-reform policy-maker will increase the probability of the reform, while strengthening incentives for the pro-reform group to remain inactive. The effect on the against-reform group's incentives to enter depends on the shape of $(1 - e)\psi''(e)$ but the bulk of the analysis remains unchanged.

Remark 10 On Menus and Communication (Redux). *Let us now investigate the consequences of allowing menus in the present context of a non-negative constraints on transfers. First, remember that those constraints are justified by the fact that the agent may refuse to pay back the principal. In other words, the agent has now available an ex post action (to refuse or not the payments in each*

---

[23] The condition for these two inequalities to be compatible is precisely $\overline{S}_1 > \frac{n_2}{1+n_2}\overline{S}_2$.

state of nature) on top of its earlier acceptance of the state-contingent outcome. The only feasible contracts consist now in a positive payment in the state of nature which is the most favored by the principal under scrutiny (depending on whether principals have congruent preferences or conflicting ones, the relevant states of nature of course differ). When restricted to a single state-contingent payment, offering menus of those is again irrelevant; the agent would always choose the highest such payments. It justifies our focus on take-it-or-leave-it offers in the first place.

8 Coalitional Behavior

A key aspect of modern politics, which has been repeatedly pointed out by several political scientists, is that as the number of active interest groups has dramatically increased over the past four decades, from 5,000 in 1955 to over 33,000 at the end of the twentieth century, distinct interest groups have often chosen to cooperate and adopt collective strategies to leverage their influence on policy-makers. For instance, Hula (1999)[24] showed that, respectively, 81.3, 79.6, and 83.3 percent of interviewed institutional members in areas like transportation, education, and civil rights issues agree on thinking that forming coalitions is the best way to be effective in politics. Accordingly, a key test of the validity of any theory of Legislative politics is whether such a theory can explain those incentives for coalition building. This section addresses this issue.

8.1 Coalition-Proof Nash Equilibria

The first concept of interest to study coalitional behavior is the recursive concept of *Coalition-Proof Nash Equilibrium* (thereafter *CPNE*). It was developed in order to account for possible joint deviations by some coalitions, requiring that such deviations should themselves be self-enforcing and immune to coalitional deviations that are themselves *CPNE* on the so reduced game among deviating groups.[25] Bernheim and Whinston (1986b) showed that the set of payoffs achieved by *CPNE* corresponds to the set of payoffs achieved through truthful equilibria of the complete information delegated common agency game. This important result has sometimes been viewed as another justification for focusing on the truthfulness criterion. Yet, the flip side of this result is

---

[24] See also the references therein.

[25] More precisely, Bernheim, Peleg, and Whinston (1986) argue that a *CPNE* belongs to the efficient frontier of equilibria that are self-enforcing, *"in the sense that no coalition can (taking the strategies of its complement as fixed) make a mutually beneficial, self-enforcing joint deviation from it"* (p. 5). The notion of *CPNE* stands thus in contrast with *Strong Nash equilibrium* (Aumann, 1959) that models coalitional deviations that are enforceable agreements.

that it also means that we should not observe any active coalitional behavior by interest groups – a rather implausible conclusion in view of the evidence reported above.

As shown in next Lemma, the same somehow disappointing result holds in our context as well.

Lemma 3 *Whether preferences are conflicting or congruent, and whether contracting is unrestricted or restricted to nonnegative transfers, all equilibria exhibited in the previous section are CPNE.*

8.2 Binding Agreements

Taken at face value, Lemma 3 suggests that there is no more scope for any collusive behavior among principals than what is already implicitly contained in the equilibrium characterization. Yet, we should acknowledge that the self-enforceability requirement *CPNE* puts stringent limits on the kind of coalitional behavior that is permitted.

In contrast, we may want to explore another polar assumption and allow groups to efficiently coordinate their contributions by signing *binding* agreements. Such a possibility can be seen as giving an upper bound on the groups' incentives to engage in coalition building. To do so, we first introduce the following definition:

Definition 5 *A Nash equilibrium of the delegated common agency game is a Merger-Proof Nash Equilibrium (MPNE in the sequel) if no enforceable deviation by any coalition reaches a strictly larger aggregate payoff for that coalition than the sum of its members' payoffs in that equilibrium.*

Said differently, an equilibrium is *MPNE* if no coalition is strictly better-off when merging and behaving as a single player who would be able to redistribute gains among its members. Although straightforward, this definition contains implicitly two requirements. First, merging does not modify the set of feasible contracts (whether those contracts are unrestricted or require nonnegative contributions). Second, principals of such merger can also prevent any further side-contracting between any subset of those and the agent. The contractual externalities that might appear, had these principals adopted a noncooperative behavior, is thus fully internalized by the merging coalition.[26] Using the

---

[26] Ray and Vohra (1997)'s concept of *equilibrium binding agreement* considers a more complex setting, where binding coalitions may split further, and where players contemplating to form a coalition anticipate the reactions of others (instead of taking as given the others' strategies, as

concept of *MPNE* to compare the scenarios with unrestricted contracting or with nonnegative payments is therefore a way to assess the potential gains that may result from coalition building.

8.2.1 Congruent Interests

In this case, the concept of *MPNE* gives a sharp contrast between the scenarios with unrestricted contracting or with nonnegative payments.

Proposition 8 *Suppose congruent preferences.*

1. *All equilibria with unrestricted contracting are MPNE.*
2. *The unique equilibrium with a nonnegativity constraint on payments is not MPNE.*

The first part of this result is intuitive. Under unrestricted contracting, the efficient effort is implemented, and the agent gets no rent when principals are congruent. Coalition building allows a proper coalition S of principals to free-ride upon others' contribution. Since the best deviation available to that coalition is still a truthful schedule of the form $\tilde{T}_S = \tilde{S}_S - C_S$, implementing the efficient effort remains optimal. Compared to the sum of the individual truthful contributions, this collective deviation would thus be valuable if and only if $C_S > C_S^D$. But given that the agent gets zero payoff, there is no scope for extracting more rent from the agent for those principals. In the frictionless world of Section 4, all efficiency gains are already exhausted through the principals' individual moves.

This result no longer holds when payments are restricted to be nonnegative. By designing contributions noncooperatively, principals exert an externality on each others, each taking into account the whole marginal agency cost of providing incentives to the common agent. A merger helps to internalize this negative externality.

To illustrate, observe that the contribution of a merger of two principals is, for instance, *always* greater than that of those principals taken separately since, thanks to a convexity property, the following inequality holds:

$$\max(\overline{S}_i - e\psi''(e), 0) + \max(\overline{S}_j - e\psi''(e), 0) < \max(\overline{S}_i + \overline{S}_j - e\psi''(e), 0) \quad \forall e.$$

Collective deviations are thus valuable because they help internalizing an incentive externality, and reducing free riding. With congruent preferences,

---

for *CPNE* or for our approach). Since our concern is more about the mere existence of gains from merging, we shall not enter into such considerations.

the introduction of the nonnegativity constraint (i.e., of real contracting frictions) creates a scope for coalition building that was absent under unrestricted contracting.

8.2.2 Conflicting Interests

Here, the same logic is at play, though in a less clear way.

Proposition 9 *Suppose conflicting preferences and n = 2.*

1. *No equilibrium, either with or without a nonnegativity constraint on payments, is MPNE.*
2. *With unrestricted contracting, all gains associated to binding coalitional agreements come from the reduction of the agent's rent.*
3. *With nonnegative payments, the gains associated to binding coalitional agreements come both from the reduction of the agent's rent and from an increase in efficiency.*

Item 1 is intuitive. With conflicting preferences, the agent obtains a rent by playing a principal against the other. By merging, the two principals no longer compete head-to-head and they can now push the agent down to its reservation payoff.

Yet, the difference between items 2 and 3 is worth noticing. With unrestricted contracting, a merger has no impact on allocative efficiency, since efficiency prevails under all configurations. On the contrary, with nonnegative payments, a merger has an effect not only on rent extraction but also on the policy decision. To see this, compare (7.5) with the modified Lindahl–Samuelson resulting from a merger between two groups, namely:

$$\overline{S}_1 - \underline{S}_2 - e\psi''(e) = \psi'(e).$$

By merging, two conflicting groups are able to induce a more favorable effort, while reducing the rent of the agent. Both allocative and distributive dimensions are at play in determining groups' incentives to build coalitions.

8.2.3 Contractual Frictions and Coalitions

Introducing contracting frictions in the relationship that each group entertains with the decision-maker, in the form of non-negativity of payments under moral hazard, therefore provides a theory of why coalitions form. Merging becomes attractive when those frictions can be collectively reduced by the merging groups. This possibility is especially clear in the case of congruent interests; a scenario where, arguably, such coalitions are likely to be easier to be built.

That coalitional behavior among groups prevails in practice certainly supports the idea that frictions between interest groups and decision-makers prevail. Without such frictions, coalitional behavior has no bite.

Of course, *MPNE* might be viewed as too strong a concept. Indeed, we have assumed that a merger of interest groups is costless; focusing thereby on the benefits of reducing agency costs with the decision-maker. Some costs of coalition formation should certainly be also introduced to get a more realistic picture of the determinants of the process of coalition building. For instance, jointly designing contributions might require communication among merging groups if their preferences are not common knowledge. Enforcing a merger may also be hard and only sustained through repeated interactions subject to opportunistic behavior. In any case, the prevalence of coalitions in practice suggests that those costs of coalition formation are second order in comparison with the benefits of reduced transaction costs of influence in the relationship with decision-makers.

9 Conclusion

In this Element, we have analyzed competition among lobbying groups as a delegated common agency model under moral hazard in a political economy environment. This study was motivated by the fact that most of the existing models of lobbying where several interest groups try to influence a single decision-maker were unable to link the allocative and redistributive aspects of lobbying and to give foundations for why some groups intervene whereas others do not, and why they might adopt collective behavior. Moral hazard may introduce frictions that respond to those weaknesses.

Summarizing, the main findings are as follows. First, under unrestricted contracting and moral hazard, all equilibria are efficient, involve active participation by all interest groups, and are obtained with truthful contributions which makes the decision-maker residual claimant for his decision. In other words, the main lessons of the complete information common agency model of lobbying competition carry over even when moral hazard matters. Yet, instead of being an equilibrium refinement as in the extent literature, truthfulness is now endogenously derived at equilibrium. The set of equilibrium payoffs can be easily characterized through a system of fundamental equations. This system is easily solved for either congruent or conflicting principals.

However, those truthful schedules require the agent to pay back interest groups in case the political outcome hurts them; an unpalatable conclusion. Introducing a more natural nonnegativity constraint on payments, interest groups only pay the decision-maker when favorable political outcomes realize. Restricting contracting possibilities in this manner implies that a moral hazard rent is now left to the policy-maker. This rent, which is viewed as costly by interest groups, is the source of significant frictions in the game of influence. The unique equilibrium found in such settings is no longer efficient. To illustrate, free riding among congruent but noncooperating interest groups may now arise. A given interest group only retains a private benefit from inducing more effort from the decision-maker but he bears all the cost of doing so in terms of moral hazard rent left to the decision-maker. Interest groups find it optimal to contribute if and only if their (marginal) benefit exceeds the (marginal) cost of the moral hazard rent. The existence of a contractual externality across principals and of some heterogeneity in their preferences are thus key to explain why some groups remain out of the political process. Then, the magnitude of allocative inefficiency and the redistribution of the aggregate surplus both depend on the endogenous set of contributing principals. This agency perspective yields some valuable insights on the Olsonian program of understanding how the size and heterogeneity of groups with similar interests determine the form of collective action. It also provides a way of explaining why some groups coalesce when entering in the political arena, while others do not.

Our framework could be extended toward several directions. A first obvious path would be to generalize the modeling of the political process, allowing maybe for a richer set of political outcomes, and possibly for various interest groups favoring different outcomes. Certainly the results of the present study would be robust but might be obtained at the cost of extra complexity.

A second quite natural extension would be to have a more micro-founded modeling of the decision-making process. For instance, several legislators may be at play simultaneously and under the influence of several lobbies. The pattern of influence links and networks which emerge in such environments should be analyzed.

Also, the cost of increasing the likelihood of a reform has been so far taken as exogenous. In a political economy setting, one certainly wants to endogenize this cost as coming from the various trade-offs that a decision-maker faces in favoring either lobbying groups or the general public.

Lastly, it would be worth to go deeper into the modeling of how coalitions of interest groups form. In particular, the nature of the contractual externalities among those principals is a key ingredient to understand why some coalitions emerge while others fail to do so – an issue certainly worth investigating.

All these questions await for further research.

Appendix A
Proofs of Main Results

Proof of Proposition 1. Direct from the text for (4.4), (4.5), and (4.7). For (4.6), note that principal i would get a payoff

$$\max_{e \in [0,1]} \left\{ \mathbb{E}\left(\tilde{S}_i + \tilde{T}_{A-i} | e\right) - \psi(e) - \max\left\{0, \max_{S \subseteq N}\left(E(\tilde{T}_S | e_S) - \psi(e_S)\right)\right\} \right\}$$

by inducing another active coalition of principals A. □

Proof of Proposition 2. This proof has three parts. In the first one, we first prove the convexity of the cooperative game among principals with characteristic form $(W_S)_{S \subseteq N}$. Second, we use that result to derive existence and payoff properties of an equilibrium where all principals are active. Third, we show that no other equilibrium where only a proper subset of principals is active can exist.

Convexity of the Cooperative Game $(W_S)_{S \subseteq N}$. We first prove an important Lemma.

Lemma A.1 *When principals have congruent preferences,*

$$W_N \geq W_K + W_{N-K}, \quad \text{for all } K \subseteq N. \tag{A.1}$$

always holds.

Proof of Lemma A.1. Observe that when principals have congruent preferences:

$$W_K = \max_{e \in [0,1]} \left\{ e\left(\sum_{i \in K} \bar{S}_i\right) - \psi(e) \right\}.$$

Now choose two effort levels e_1 and e_2 and define $\hat{e} = \max\{e_1, e_2\}$. The following inequalities hold:

$$\hat{e}\left(\sum_{i \in N} \bar{S}_i\right) = \hat{e}\left(\sum_{i \in K} \bar{S}_i\right) + \hat{e}\left(\sum_{i \in N-K} \bar{S}_i\right) \geq e_1\left(\sum_{i \in K} \bar{S}_i\right) + e_2\left(\sum_{i \in N-K} \bar{S}_i\right), \tag{A.2}$$

and

$$\psi(\hat{e}) = \psi(\max\{e_1, e_2\}) \leq \psi(e_1) + \psi(e_2). \tag{A.3}$$

Gathering (A.2) and (A.3) yields

$$\hat{e}\left(\sum_{i \in N} \bar{S}_i\right) - \psi(\hat{e}) \geq \left(e_1\left(\sum_{i \in K} \bar{S}_i\right) - \psi(e_1)\right) + \left(e_2\left(\sum_{i \in N-K} \bar{S}_i\right) - \psi(e_2)\right).$$

Therefore,

$$W_N \geq \left(e_1 \left(\sum_{i \in K} \overline{S_i}\right) - \psi(e_1)\right) + \left(e_2 \left(\sum_{i \in N-K} \overline{S_i}\right) - \psi(e_2)\right), \text{ for all } (e_1, e_2).$$

Finally, (A.1) is obtained by taking max on the r.h.s. $\qquad\square$

Equilibrium Payoffs When All Principals Are Active

Consider now the system of linear inequalities

$$C_N^D = W_N, \tag{A.4}$$
$$C_K^D \leq W_N - W_{N-K}. \tag{A.5}$$

This system is equivalent to:

$$C_N^D = W_N, \tag{A.6}$$
$$C_K^D \geq W_K. \tag{A.7}$$

Solutions to (A.6) and (A.7) are also solutions to (4.14). This system defines a nonempty set of vectors $(C_i^D)_{1 \leq i \leq n}$ whenever (A.1) holds. The set of equilibrium payoffs $(C_i^D)_{1 \leq i \leq n}$ can thus be identified with the core of a cooperative game with characteristic form $(W_S)_{S \subseteq N}$. From Lemma A.1, this game is convex and its core is nonempty (Shapley, 1971). Provided that no principal wants to deviate by inducing a smaller coalition than the grand one, this shows that there exist equilibria of the delegated common agency game where all principals are active.

Using (A.6) and (A.7), note also that

$$C_i^D \geq W_i > 0. \tag{A.8}$$

Hence, each principal gets a positive payoff in an equilibrium where all principals are active.

The grand-coalition emerges

Let us now show that a principal does not want to deviate by inducing another coalition of active principals than the grand coalition. For this, we must check that condition (4.6) holds. This means:

$$W_N - \sum_{j \neq i} C_j \geq W_S - \sum_{j \neq i, j \in S} C_j$$

for any S such that $\{i\} \subseteq S \subseteq N$. This can be written alternatively as:

$$W_N - C_N \geq W_S - C_S, \quad \forall S \subset N, \tag{A.9}$$

where $(C_i^D)_{1 \leq n}$ satisfies (A.6) and (A.7).

But using (A.7), (A.9) clearly holds and thus no principal wants to deviate by inducing a proper coalition.

No Other Equilibrium with a Proper Coalition of Active Principals Exists
Denote by A^* $\subset$ N a proper coalition that would emerge in such a putative equilibrium. The condition for A^* to be the set of active principals is thus that for any principal $i \in A^*$:

$$\mathbb{E}\left(\tilde{S}_i + \tilde{T}_{A^*-\{i\}}|e_{A^*}\right) - \psi(e_{A^*}) \geq \max_{\{i\}\subseteq A\subseteq N}\left\{\mathbb{E}\left(\tilde{S}_i + \tilde{T}_{A-\{i\}}|e_A\right) - \psi(e_A)\right\}.$$

(A.10)

For principals $i \notin A^*$, this formula must be replaced by

$$\mathbb{E}\left(\tilde{S}_i|e_{A^*}\right) \geq \max_{\{i\}\subseteq A\subseteq N}\left\{\mathbb{E}\left(\tilde{S}_i + \tilde{T}_{A-\{i\}}|e_A\right) - \psi(e_A)\right.$$
$$\left. - \max\left\{0, \max_{S\subseteq N}\left(\mathbb{E}(\tilde{T}_S|e_S) - \psi(e_S)\right)\right\}\right\}.$$

(A.11)

Proceeding as done in the text when the grand-coalition forms, any principal i in A^* offers necessarily a truthful schedule $\tilde{t}_i = \tilde{S}_i - C_i^{D'}$ for some $C_i^{D'}$.

Consider now $i_0 \notin A^*$. Such i_0 exists by definition of A^*. This principal gets thus a payoff $\hat{C}_{i_0} = \mathbb{E}\left(\tilde{S}_i|e_{A^*}\right)$ in such equilibrium.

Let us denote also by U_{A^*} the agent's equilibrium payoff. From the fact that principals in A^* want to extract as much as possible from the agent, we have:

$$W_{A^*} - C_{A^*} = U_{A^*}.$$

(A.12)

Suppose now that principal i_0 deviates by offering a truthful strategy

$$\hat{\tilde{t}}_{i_0} = \tilde{S}_{i_0} - C_{i_0}$$

with C_{i_0} being computed so that the agent is indifferent between the putative equilibrium, and accepting offers from principals in $A^* \cup \{i_0\}$ (producing then the corresponding optimal effort $e_{A^*\cup\{i_0\}}$).

We have to distinguish two cases:

1. When proposed with the new contract $\hat{\tilde{t}}_{i_0}$, the agent accepts all contracts proposed by principals in $A^* \cup \{i_0\}$, and no other one. Such a deviation then gives

$$W_{A^*\cup\{i_0\}} - C_{A^*} - U_{A^*} = W_{A^*\cup\{i_0\}} - W_{A^*}$$

to principal i_0. But, by definition,

$$W_{A^*\cup\{i_0\}} > e_{A^*}(\overline{S}_{A^*} + \overline{S}_{i_0}) - \psi(e_{A^*}) = W_{A^*} + \hat{C}_{i_0}.$$

(A.13)

This shows that principal i_0 has one deviation which improves his payoff (at least weakly) and induces his participation.

2. The new contract, by raising the agent's effort, now makes it worthwhile for the agent to accept other contracts that he previously preferred to refuse. Let us denote A^d the set of principals different from i_0 whose offers are now accepted. Since we are considering a putative equilibrium where some of these contracts are refused, there is no reason to assume that they all follow truthful strategies. They are of the form $(\bar{t}_k, \underline{t}_k)_{k \in A^d}$. Still, the key point is the following. Whatever the set of contracts accepted by the agent, $\hat{\tilde{t}}_{i_0}$ will be part of it. Otherwise, A^* would fail being an equilibrium. Since $\hat{\tilde{t}}_{i_0}$ makes the agent residual claimant for $\tilde{S}_{i_0}$, the payoff of principal i_0 will be C_{i_0}, whatever the optimal effort $e_{A^d \cup \{i_0\}}$ chosen by the agent. The deviation is again profitable to principal i_0. Hence, there cannot exist an equilibrium with a proper coalition forming. □

Proof of Proposition 3. First, we again analyze the properties of the cooperative game between principals. Then, we analyze payoffs in a putative equilibrium of the delegated common agency game where all principals are active. We finally prove that such an equilibrium exists and is unique.

Subadditivity of the Characteristic Function. For $n = 2$ and conflicting preferences, we have

$$W_2 = \max_{e \in [0,1]} \{(1 - e)\underline{S}_2 - \psi(e)\} = \underline{S}_2,$$

$$W_1 = \max_{e \in [0,1]} \{e\bar{S}_1 - \psi(e)\} > \max_{e \in [0,1]} \{e(\bar{S}_1 - \underline{S}_2) - \psi(e)\}$$

$$= W_{12} - W_2.$$

Hence, we get

$$W_{12} < W_1 + W_2. \tag{A.14}$$

Payoffs When the Grand-Coalition Emerges. Let us turn to (4.14) and observe that the only possibility for solving this system is now

$$W_{12} - C_1^D - C_2^D = W_i - C_i^D, \quad \text{for } i = 1, 2. \tag{A.15}$$

Therefore, we obtain

$$C_i^D = W_{12} - W_{-i} > 0 \tag{A.16}$$

and the agent gets also a nonnegative payoff equal to

$$W_{12} - C_1^D - C_2^D = W_1 + W_2 - W_{12} > 0. \tag{A.17}$$

Hence, if an equilibrium of the delegated common agency game where all principals are active exists, it gives necessarily a payoff C_i^D as defined in (A.16) to principal i.

Such an equilibrium in fact exists. Using (4.6), it must be that, for principal 1

$$W_{12} - C_2^D \geq W_1$$

and for principal 2

$$W_{12} - C_1^D \geq W_2,$$

and clearly those conditions hold as equalities by definition of C_i^D.

No Equilibrium with a Proper Coalition of Active Principals Exists.

Let consider the case where principal 1 (the dominant one) would be the sole contributing principal. We denote e_1 the corresponding effort.

Equation (A.11) still applies here, but for such putative equilibrium. This equilibrium gives payoffs C_1' to principal 1 and $\hat{C}_2^D = (1 - e_1)\underline{S}_2$ to the inactive principal 2.

From (A.11) for principal 1, we get:

$$W_1 \geq W_{12} - C_2' \tag{A.18}$$

for some C_2' corresponding to the truthful strategy proposed by principal 2 (and rejected by the agent).

Using the fact that the agent's participation constraint is binding at equilibrium, we have:

$$W_1 - C_1' = \max\{0, W_2 - C_2', W_{12} - C_1' - C_2'\}. \tag{A.19}$$

Finally, from (A.11) for principal 2, we get:

$$\hat{C}_2 \geq W_2 - \max\{0, W_1 - C_1'\} \tag{A.20}$$

to prevent a deviation by principal 2 such that only himself contracts with the agent and

$$\hat{C}_2 \geq W_{12} - C_1' - \max\{0, W_1 - C_1'\} \tag{A.21}$$

to prevent a deviation by principal 2 such that the agent contracts with both principals.

First, note that, by definition of e^D,

$$W_{12} > W_1 + \hat{C}_2. \tag{A.22}$$

But, in equilibrium, necessarily $W_1 \geq C_1'$ from (A.19). Inserting into (A.21), we obtain a contradiction with (A.22).

The case of a putative equilibrium where only principal 2 contracts with the agent can be eliminated similarly. □

Proof of Lemma 2. First, we can rule out the case where a principal i is inactive at equilibrium. Indeed, the fact that transfers have to be nonnegative means that the agent will accept any contract with a positive contribution associated to at least one outcome. An inactive principal will therefore offer $\bar{t}_i = t_i = 0$.

Going back to the case of unrestricted contracting, the contribution offered by a principal i, and the effort by the agent, still have to satisfy conditions (4.1) and (4.2).

If neither (4.1) nor the constraint that $\tilde{t}_i \geq 0$ are binding, principal i can increase his payoff by decreasing the payments $\tilde{t}_i$ for all outcomes $\tilde{S}_i$ by an amount ϵ small enough, still satisfying those constraints while improving his payoff. One of those constraints must therefore be binding.

If (4.1) is the binding constraint, then Lemma 1 still applies, as do the necessary conditions (4.8) and (4.9). The optimal contract proposed by principal i should thus satisfy equality (4.12), where $C_i^D \geq 0$, otherwise principal i would be better off by proposing the null contract. This is only possible for $\tilde{t}_i = C_i^D = 0$ when $\tilde{S}_i = 0$.

If $\tilde{t}_i \geq 0$ is the binding constraint, then it is clear that it will be binding for the transfer associated to $\tilde{S}_i = 0$. Otherwise, principal i would be strictly better off by offering no contract. □

Proof of Proposition 4. Using a necessary first-order condition and a fixed-point requirement for the self-generating problem (P^{SE}) yields the expression of the (interior) equilibrium effort as (5.14). This equilibrium effort is of course unique.

Reciprocally, let us consider the payments $\bar{t}_i^I$ such that (5.14) holds. Those payments are also such that

$$\bar{S}_i - \bar{t}_i^I = \frac{1}{n}(\bar{S}_N - \bar{T}^I).$$

Thus, we get

$$\bar{S}_i + \bar{T}_{-i}^I = \frac{1}{n}\bar{S}_N + \frac{n-1}{n}\bar{T}^I.$$

Inserting into the maximand of $(P_i^I)'$ shows that principal i's optimization problem boils down to (P^{SE}). This proves that the necessary conditions for an equilibrium are also sufficient. □

Proof of Propositions 5 and 6. We use the fact that there is no loss of generality in assuming that no principal views his offer being rejected (some offers may be null of course). For the sake of clarity, we then turn to the identification between equilibria with a grand-coalition where some principals make null offers and equilibria with a proper coalition where some offers would be rejected.

Equilibrium Payoffs When All Principals Are Active.

We now solve $(P_i^D)'$. Two cases must be distinguished depending on whether (6.2) binds or not.

Consider principals for which it does not bind. Given that $\psi' > 0$, $\psi'' > 0$, and $\psi''' \geq 0$, principal i's objective function is strictly concave and the effort optimally induced in equilibrium solves:

$$\overline{S}_i + \overline{T}_{-i} = \psi'(e) + e\psi''(e). \tag{A.23}$$

Condition (6.2) holds whenever principal i's contribution is nonnegative, that is, when

$$\overline{t}_i = \overline{S}_i - e\psi''(e) \geq 0. \tag{A.24}$$

Let us take conditions (A.23) for all principals active in equilibrium (denote A this set) and sum those conditions to get

$$\overline{S}_A + (|A| - 1)\overline{T}_A = |A|(\psi'(e) + e\psi''(e)),$$

where $|A|$ denotes the cardinal of A.

Then using (5.11) yields:

$$\overline{S}_A = \psi'(e) + |A|e\psi''(e). \tag{A.25}$$

From (A.24), principal i is active if and only if

$$\overline{S}_i > e\psi''(e),$$

where e solves (A.25). From this, we immediately deduce that A is of the form $\{n - k + 1, \ldots, n\}$ and $|A| = k$ is the solution to (A.25).

Note that an alternative formulation for the equilibrium condition is:

$$\sum_{i=1}^{n} \max(S_i - e\psi''(e), 0) = \psi'(e). \tag{A.26}$$

The l.h.s. of (A.26) is decreasing in e, whereas the r.h.s. is increasing. Hence, the equilibrium is unique.

The Grand-Coalition Emerges (with Possibly Some Contributions Being Null)

To show that no principal wants to induce another coalition of active principals, first define

$$V_i(T) = \max_{e\in[0,1]} e(\bar{S}_i + T - \psi'(e))$$

subject to $\psi'(e) \geq T$.

When the constraint does not bind, the solution is achieved for $e_i(T)$ (which increases with T) such that

$$\psi'(e_i(T)) + e_i(T)\psi''(e_i(T)) = \bar{S}_i + T,$$

and it does not bind when $\psi'(e_i(T)) > T$ or $\bar{S}_i > e_i(T)\psi''(e_i(T))$ or, alternatively, for $T < T_i^*$ for some T_i^*. Otherwise, that is, for $T \geq T_i^*$, the optimal effort is $e_i(T)$ (which increases also with T) such that $\psi'(e_i(T)) = T$. In fact, we can write $V_i(T) = e_i^2(T)\psi''(e_i(T))$ for $T < T_i^*$ and $V_i(T) = \tilde{e}_i(T)\bar{S}_i$ for $T \geq T_i^*$. Thus $V_i(T)$ increases with T. Because each principal makes a nonnegative contribution,

$$V_i(\bar{T}_N) \geq V_i(\bar{T}_S)$$

for any S such that $\{i\} \subseteq S \subset N$. This means that principal i never wants to induce a deviation where some offers are rejected.

Identification. Consider an equilibrium with a proper coalition A^* of principals whose offers are accepted. Let $i_0 \notin A^*$. Clearly, principal i_0 could as well offer a null contribution which would be accepted. One can thus identify equilibria with a grand-coalition forming and some null contributions being made with equilibria with a proper coalition forming. ☐

Proof of Propositions 7. Let us first solve (P_1^D) by neglecting constraint (7.4). (P_1^D) amounts then to

$$(P_1^D)' : \quad \max_{e\in[0,1]} e(\bar{S}_1 - \underline{t}_2 - \psi'(e)).$$

By concavity of the objective function, we get the first-order condition

$$\bar{S}_1 - \underline{t}_2 = \psi'(e) + e\psi''(e). \tag{A.27}$$

Note that the induced effort is positive as long as $\bar{S}_1 > \underline{t}_2$. In fact, we will show next that $\underline{t}_2 < \underline{S}_2$ at equilibrium so that this latter condition is indeed satisfied.

Together (A.27) and (7.1) imply

$$\bar{t}_1 = \bar{S}_1 - e\psi''(e) = \underline{t}_2 + \psi'(e) > \underline{t}_2$$

for any positive level of effort so that (7.4) holds. Moreover, because $\underline{t}_2 \geq 0$, we have $\bar{t}_1 = \bar{S}_1 - e\psi''(e) > 0$ for a positive level of effort being implemented in equilibrium.

Let us turn to principal 2's problem (P_2^D). First, note that the participation constraint can be written as:

$$\underline{t}_2 + R(\phi(\bar{t}_1 - \underline{t}_2)) \geq R(\phi(\bar{t}_1)), \tag{A.28}$$

where $\phi = \psi'^{-1}$. Note that $R'(\phi(x)) = \phi(x) < 1$ so that (A.28) amounts to (7.3).

Neglecting for the moment constraint (7.3), (P_2^D) can be rewritten as:

$$(P_2^D)' : \quad \max_{e \in [0,1]} (1 - e)(\underline{S}_2 - \bar{t}_1 + \psi'(e)).$$

This objective function is concave when $(1 - e)\psi'(e)$ is itself concave. The first-order condition for effort is then

$$\underline{S}_2 - \bar{t}_1 = -\psi'(e) + (1 - e)\psi''(e). \tag{A.29}$$

If follows from (A.27) that principal 2's contribution is positive as long as

$$\underline{S}_2 > (1 - e)\psi''(e). \tag{A.30}$$

Using (7.1), (A.27), and (A.29), we finally get

$$\bar{S}_1 - \underline{S}_2 = \psi'(e^D) + (2e^D - 1)\psi''(e^D), \tag{A.31}$$

as long as $\underline{S}_2 > (1 - e^D)\psi''(e^D)$ and

$$\bar{S}_1 = \psi'(e^D) + e^D\psi''(e^D) \tag{A.32}$$

otherwise. Summarizing, we get (7.5). When $(1 - e)\psi'(e)$ is concave, the r.h.s. in (A.31) is increasing, while the one in (A.32) is always so. The equilibrium is thus unique.

The Grand-Coalition Necessarily Emerges. Contributions by each principal being always positive, none of them has a deviation which induces the agent to accept only one of the offered contract. The agent gets always more rent by taking both contracts.   □

Proof of Lemma 3. Conflicting Preferences. Equilibria with conflicting preferences only involve two principals in our setting. In this case a Nash Equilibrium is a *CPNE* if and only if it is not Pareto dominated by another equilibrium. Since equilibria are unique, it is obviously the case.

Congruent Preferences with Nonnegativity Payments. Given an equilibrium $(\{t_1^D, \ldots t_n^D\}, e^D)$, and a subset of principals $K \subset N$, we consider the game Γ_K as the game of common agency between principals belonging to K, contributions $\bar{T}_{N-K}$ being held constant.

It is enough to show that every Γ_K has a unique equilibrium. To do so, let us consider $K \subset N$, and call $A \subseteq K$ the set of active principals in an equilibrium $(\{\bar{t}_i\}_{i \in K}, e)$ of Γ_K.

Reasoning like in the proof of Proposition 5, (A.23)–(A.25) yield

$$\bar{S}_A + \bar{T}^D_{-K} = \psi(e) + |A|e\psi''(e), \tag{A.33}$$

with $\bar{T}^D_{-K} = \sum_{j \in N-K} \max\left(\bar{S}_j - e^D\psi''(e^D), 0\right)$. Accordingly we can rewrite (A.33) as

$$\sum_{i \in K} \max\left(\bar{S}_i - e\psi''(e), 0\right) + \sum_{j \in N-K} \max\left(\bar{S}_j - e^D\psi''(e^D), 0\right) = \psi'(e).$$

This equation has a unique solution which is $e = e^D$. This ends this part of the proof.

Congruent Preferences under Unrestricted Contracting.

Because contributions are truthful and the equilibrium effort is first best, e^D, the description of the game boils down to the set of fees. Let thus $E^D = (C_1^D, \ldots, C_n^D)$ be an equilibrium of the unconstrained delegated common agency game.

We adapt the previous notations, denoting by $\Gamma_K(T_{-K})$ the restriction of the game to the principals in K and the agent, when principals in $N - K$ offer a set of truthful contributions $\tilde{T}_{-K} = \{\tilde{t}_j\}_{j \in N-K}$ where $\tilde{t}_j = \tilde{S}_j - C - j^D$. For $K \subseteq N$, we denote $T_K^* \equiv (\{C_i^*\}_{i \in K})$ the restriction of E^D to the principals in K, and by $E_K^* \equiv (\{C_i^*\}_{i \in K}, e^*)$ the same restriction including the agent's action.

We follow the definition and terms of Bernheim, Peleg, and Whinston (1986, p. 6), recalled in Bernheim and Whinston (1986b, p. 16).

For $k \in \{1, \ldots, n\}$, let denote R_k the proposition that for all $J \subseteq N$ with $|J| \leq k$, E_J^* is a *CPNE* of the game $\Gamma_J(T_{-J}^*)$.

R_1 is obviously satisfied. Let assume R_{k-1} is true, for $k \leq n$. Now, let us consider $K \subseteq N$ with $|K| = k$, and prove that E_K^* is a CPNE of the game $\Gamma_K(T_{K,J}^*)$.

First, we have to show that E_K^* is self-enforcing. To see this, consider any $J \subset K$. The important thing is that $\left(\Gamma_K(T_{-K}^*)\right)_J(T_{K-J}^*) = \Gamma_J(T_{-J}^*)$. Applying R_{k-1}, we thus have that for any $J \subset K$, E_J^* is a CPNE in the restriction of $\Gamma_K(T_{N-K}^*)$ to J and the agent.

Second, we have to show that the payoffs in $\Gamma_K(T_{-K}^*)$ when principals in K play E_K^* are not Pareto dominated by another self-enforcing Nash equilibrium. To do so, we prove the stronger proposition that they are undominated by any other equilibrium.

Under delegated common agency, the set of principals in K cannot let the agent with a negative payoff. The maximum payoff V_K they can get as a whole is therefore bounded by the aggregate surplus of the coalition they form with the agent, potentially excluding some principals in $N - K$:

$$V_K \leq \max_{S \subseteq N-K} \left\{ \max_{e \geq 0} \left\{ e \left(\bar{S}_K + \bar{S}_S \right) - \psi(e) - C_S^* \right\} \right\}. \tag{A.34}$$

Assume that K can increase its aggregate payoff by excluding some other principals. In this case, there exists $S \subseteq N - K$ such that

$$W_{K \cup S} - C_j^* > W_N - C_{N-K}^*.$$

This implies that $W_N - W_{K \cup S} < \sum_{j \in N \setminus (K \cup S)} C_j^*$. But this contradicts condition (A.5) for E^* to be an equilibrium.

Therefore, using (A.34) and (A.6),

$$V_K \leq W_N - C_{N-K}^* = C_K^*.$$

Payoffs obtained with E_K^* are Pareto dominated by no equilibrium of $\Gamma_K(T_{-K}^*)$. This proves R_k.

Applying induction up to R_n, E^* is a *CPNE* of the delegated common agency game. □

Proof of Propositions 8 and 9. Congruent preferences with unrestricted contracting. Let $(C_1^D, \ldots, C_n^D)$ be the principals' payoffs in any equilibrium. For all $S \subseteq N$, equation (A.6) holds.

Consider a coalition $S \subseteq N$ of principals. Proceeding as in the proof of Proposition 2, the best strategy of that deviating coalition is to offer a truthful schedule:

$$\tilde{T}_{iS} = \tilde{S}_{iS} - C_S.$$

By inducing the agent to accept its offer as well as those of a subset $K \subseteq N_S$, the coalition can obtain a payoff

$$W_{S \cup K} - C_K^D.$$

But for all such K, (A.7) implies that

$$C_S = W_{S \cup K} - C_K^D \leq W_{S \cup K} + W_{N \setminus (S \cup K)} - C_K^D - C_{N \setminus (S \cup K)}.$$

Lemma A.1 implies that the r.h.s. is smaller than $W_N - \sum_{i \in N-S} C_i^D$. Comparing with (A.6), no merger is strictly profitable.

Congruent Preferences with Nonnegative Payments. The proof is obvious from the text, since

$$\max(\bar{S}_i - e\psi''(e), 0) + \max(\bar{S}_j - e\psi''(e), 0) < \max(\bar{S}_i + \bar{S}_j - e\psi''(e), 0).$$

Conflicting Preferences with Unrestricted Contracting. If the two principals design their contract separately, each one gets a payoff of $C_i^D = W_{12} - W_{-i}$, while the agent gets a rent $W_1 + W_2 - W_{12}$. If they merge, they will still maximize the payoff of the grand coalition they form with the agent, but pushing the agent to his reservation payoff. The payoff of the merged entity is $C_S = W_{12} < W_1 + W_2$. But $C_1^D + C_2^D = 2W_{12} - W_1 - W_2 < W_{12}$.

Conflicting Preferences with Nonnegative Payments. Since the merged coalition can always reproduce the competitive outcome, it is enough to show that it has new options. Consider the unique equilibrium of the game, with an effort e^D. Two cases have to be distinguished.

- If $\max\{\underline{S}_2 - (1 - e^D)\psi''(e^D), 0\} = 0$, then $\bar{t}_1 = \psi'(e^D)$, $\underline{t}_2 = 0$, and the implemented effort satisfies $\bar{S}_1 - e^D\psi''(e^D) = \psi'(e^D)$. By merging, the coalition could do better, by implementing its favorite decision defined by

$$\bar{S}_1 - \underline{S}_2 - e^m\psi''(e^m) = \psi'(e^m).$$

- If $\max\{\underline{S}_2 - (1 - e^D)\psi''(e^D), 0\} > 0$, then by setting $\bar{t}_1^m = \bar{t}_1 - \underline{t}_2$ and $\underline{t}_2 = 0$, the merged coalition can get the same decision at a strictly lower cost. $\square$

Appendix B
Risk Aversion

An alternative alley to generate frictions and contractual inefficiencies between each interest group and the common policy-maker would be to introduce some degree of risk aversion on the agent's side. Then, taking stock of the lessons of the seminal works of Mirrlees (1976), Holmstrom (1979) and Grossman and Hart (1983), we know that each bilateral relationship between an interest group and this policy-maker inherits of a well-known trade-off between incentives and insurance.[1] Making the policy-maker residual claimant is no longer optimal for each interest group and contributions now fail to be truthful. Dixit (1996) already stressed such a result in a model of intrinsic common agency, that is, when all groups are supposed to necessarily interact with the policy-maker. As discussed in Martimort (2007, 2018), models of lobbying do not have such feature. The policy-maker is always free to accept only a subset of offers; a scenario which has been coined as *delegated common agency* (Bernheim and Whinston, 1986b). With delegated common agency, contractual externalities across congruent principals again induce a free riding problem that might be so strong that some of the interest groups are left apart from the political process.

On the Principals' Side

The analysis of Section 4 carries over immediately to the case where principals are risk averse and have thus a demand for insurance. Indeed, the truthful schedules not only provide to the agent first-best incentives to exert an effort but also give full insurance to the principals, insulating them from the risk of a political outcome that does not please them. With unrestricted contracting, the political process not only achieves efficiency but also provides insurance to the various groups that intervene.

On the Agent's Side

In this section, we briefly sketch a model which shows that the lessons of Section 4 somehow carry over to that environment although they need to be somewhat modified to take into account a contractual externality which is very similar to that viewed in Section 6.

To this end, we slightly modify the framework and look at the case where the political outcomes on which contribution schedules can be conditioned is

---

[1] See Laffont and Martimort (2002, ch. 4) for a textbook treatment.

a continuous variables y linked to the agent's effort e and to a noise ε which is normally distributed $N(0, \sigma^2)$ through the simple relationship:

$$y = e + \varepsilon.$$

The agent has a $CARA$ utility function with a risk aversion coefficient r and a quadratic disutility of effort $\psi(e) = \frac{e^2}{2}$. The continuous variables y can for instance be viewed as the price level of a regulated good when decision on this price is affected by the decision-maker effort but also by some noise reflecting perhaps the extent of other political pressures coming from other (unmodeled) groups and the general public.

To simplify, we assume that principal i has linear preferences given by

$$V_i = b_i y - t_i(y), \quad \text{for} \quad i \in \{1, \ldots, n\},$$

where $t_i(y)$ is the contribution he offers to the decision-maker. The parameter b_i is positive (resp. negative) if principal i enjoys (resp. is hurt by) a higher price for the good. To simplify the number of cases in the analysis, we assume that all principals have congruent preferences, with $b_i > 0$ for $i \in \{1, \ldots, n\}$.

This linear-normal environment can be viewed as a reduced form for a dynamic agency model, and it is well-known that linear contracts of the form $t_i(y) = a_i y - C_i$ are indeed optimal in such environment.[2] Accordingly, we restrict principals' contract to such linear schemes.

Given a coalition S of principals, let us denote by a_S the aggregate piece rate and by C_S the corresponding aggregate fixed fee. The aggregate contribution received by the agent is thus $a_S y - C_S$ and the certainty-equivalent of his random payoff if he exerts effort e can be written as:

$$a_S e - \frac{e^2}{2} - \frac{r\sigma^2}{2} a_S^2 - C_S.$$

The optimal effort supply is given by

$$e = a_S.$$

The corresponding certainty-equivalent of the agent's payoff becomes:

$$\frac{(1 - r\sigma^2)}{2} a_S^2 - C_S.$$

We will again proceed as in Section 4. First, we write the necessary conditions for an equilibrium where all principals are active to emerge. We shall

---

[2] See Holmstrom and Milgrom (1987) in the case of a single principal. Of course, the same reasoning carries over to the case of multiple principals. Being given that all other principals offer linear schemes, principal i finds it optimal to also offer a linear contribution schedule.

then check that there cannot exist any equilibrium where a proper coalition only emerges.

When all principals are active, principal i's best response is solution to the following problem:

(P_i^D) : $\max_{\{e, a_i, C_i\}} (b_i - a_i)e + C_i$ subject to

$$e = a_N, \tag{B.1}$$

and

$$\frac{(1 - r\sigma^2)}{2} a_N^2 - C_N \geq \max \left\{ 0, \max_{S \subset N} \left\{ \frac{(1 - r\sigma^2)}{2} a_S^2 - C_S \right\} \right\}. \tag{B.2}$$

Constraint (B.1) is the agent's incentive constraint when facing n principals. Constraint (B.2) indicates that the agent takes all offers rather than any other subset. Of course, (B.2) is necessarily binding at the optimum of (P_i^D) since each principal i wants to decrease the fee C_i^D he offers as much as possible.

We now introduce the following assumption which means that there is enough homogeneity among principals' preferences:[3]

$$b_i \geq \frac{r\sigma^2}{1 + nr\sigma^2} B_N \quad \forall i. \tag{B.3}$$

Proposition B.1 *Assume that uncertainty is small enough, $r\sigma^2 < 1$, and that Assumption (B.3) holds.*

1. *All equilibria of the delegated common agency game are such that all principals are active.*
2. *In any of those equilibria, the equilibrium piece rate parameters a_i^D are strictly less than the marginal valuation of the principals:*

$$a_i^D = b_i - \frac{r\sigma^2}{1 + nr\sigma^2} B_N < b_i. \tag{B.4}$$

3. *The agent's equilibrium payoff is zero. The equilibrium fixed fees $(C_i^D)_{1 \leq i \leq n}$ solve the system of equations:*

$$\frac{(1 - r\sigma^2)}{2} \left(\frac{B_N}{1 + nr\sigma^2} \right)^2 - C_N^D = 0$$

$$= \max_{S \subset N} \left\{ \frac{(1 - r\sigma^2)}{2} \left(B_S - \frac{r\sigma^2 |S|}{1 + nr\sigma^2} B_N \right)^2 - C_S^D \right\}. \tag{B.5}$$

---

[3] This assumption ensures interior solutions to the principals' optimization problems.

When the agent is risk averse, the marginal contribution offered by each principal is no longer truthful. As it can be seen from (B.4), this marginal contribution is indeed deflated to account for the agency cost that prevails in this moral hazard scenario. This distortion, which is familiar from the moral hazard model with *CARA* preferences and normal shocks, is proportional to the agent's degree of risk aversion r and to the noise σ^2 on performances. It becomes now costly for each principal to let the agent bear all risk because of a risk-premium necessary to induce the agent to accept this principal's contract. This principal reduces this risk-premium by making the agent's reward less sensitive to the realized outcome.

When principals design their offers noncooperatively, they do not take into account the impact of the other principals' offers on the necessary risk reduction. As a result of this uncoordinated choice of the piece rate parameters in the agent's contracts, the agent bears very little risk and his incentives to exert effort are weakened. This is a standard contractual externality among principals that arises in a moral hazard framework when agency costs matter.[4]

This externality is similar to that stressed in Section 6, although the nature of agency cost differs. When payments are restricted to be nonnegative, the problem of each principal is to extract the agent's rent whereas, under risk aversion, each principal only provides partial insurance for incentive purposes.

The consequences of this externality, and how severe is the departure from the situation of risk neutrality, depend on the degree of homogeneity among principals. When there is enough homogeneity across principals and (B.3) holds, and modulo the modifications of the slopes of the contribution schedules coming from the agency problem under risk aversion, the characterization of the equilibrium fees $(C_i^D)_{1 \leq i \leq n}$ and thus of the principals' equilibrium payoffs unfold almost as in Section 4. A noticeable difference is that the size of uncertainty borne by the agent affects the structure of the solution. We show in the proof of Proposition B.1 that the fixed fees that principals use in any equilibrium of the delegated common agency game can be identified with the core of a cooperative game among principals having characteristic form $\frac{(1-r\sigma^2)}{2} \left(B_S - \frac{r\sigma^2 |S|}{1+nr\sigma^2} B_N \right)^2$. That cooperative game is indeed *convex* only when $r\sigma^2 < 1$.[5] The facts that there is full extraction of the agent's rent in equilibrium and that all principals want to be active players follow then from this property.

---

[4] Dixit (1996) already made this point in a model with intrinsic common agency and different principals contracting on different signal of the agent's array of efforts.

[5] A remark is in order here. Under unrestricted contracting and risk neutrality, those fixed fees are also the principals' equilibrium payoffs in the delegated common agency game. Under risk aversion instead, that cooperative game is more artificial since the equilibrium payoffs in the delegated common agency game differ from the fixed fees offered. Indeed, each principal offers marginal incentives which differ from his own marginal valuation for the agent's services.

The analysis of the game under risk aversion is thus somewhat similar to the case of risk neutrality modulo some distortions in the slopes of the incentive schemes and restrictions on the underlying uncertainty. The distorted slopes of the contribution schedules capture the existing incentive externality. Fixed fees are used to redistribute what is now a second-best surplus among the principals.

When heterogeneity becomes more pronounced and Assumption (B.3) no longer holds anymore, the situation with risk aversion departs more drastically from the one in Section 3. Indeed, it may now be the case that free riding is so severe that some groups are now willing to offer *negative* piece rates, thus providing the agent with an incentive to *decrease* his effort, in exchange for a fixed fee $C_i^D < 0$. In other words, such groups prefer to free ride on the other principals offering incentives for a high effort, while choosing to make the provision of insurance the dominant feature of their own strategy.

Though all principals have congruent preferences, some of them act as if they were actually competing with conflicting ones. In such a situation, the agent may get a rent in the case all principals are active. But in this case, some principals will now prefer to form a proper coalition, excluding some free riders from the set of contracting principals. The situation will come much closer to the one in Section 6, with only a subset of groups being active, some principals offering instead no contribution at all.

Proposition B.2 *Suppose Assumption (B.3) does not hold. There exists $\alpha \in (\frac{1}{2}, 1)$ such that, if $r\sigma^2 \leq \alpha$, in any equilibrium, some principals remain inactive.*

Example B.1 *To illustrate what precedes, consider the following situation: $n = 2$, $b_1 = 1$, $b_2 = 5$, and $r\sigma^2 = 1/2$.*

Assuming that both principals are active at equilibrium, there exists a putative unique equilibrium $(a_1^D, C_1^D) = (-\frac{1}{2}, -\frac{13}{16})$ and $(a_2^D, C_2^D) = (\frac{7}{2}, \frac{37}{16})$. Though the two principals have congruent preferences, this situation exhibits the properties of a game with conflicting interests. In particular, the agent now gets a positive payoff.

But this situation cannot be an equilibrium. By infinitesimally increasing his piece rate $a_2 = \frac{7}{2} + \epsilon$ principal 2 will break the agent's indifference, and induce him to accept only his offer, while rejecting the one by principal 1. This is the case because the agent's payoff exhibits increasing returns to scale as a function of the total piece rate.

In all the possible equilibria of the game, only principal 2 is active. For such a situation to be an equilibrium, principal 2 has to design his contribution in such a way that the best response for principal 1 is $a_1^D = 0$. This is achieved *for $a_2 = 2$. Being indifferent between entering or not, principal 1 can propose any contract, as long as it is not accepted. Such a contract must play a role of deterrence: Principal 1 proposes a contract with a strongly negative piece rate, designed such that principal 2 cannot increase a_2, as he wished to, without having the agent now accepting both offers. An example of such an equilibrium is offered by $(a_1^D, C_1^D) = (-10, -17)$ and $(a_2^D, C_2^D) = (2, 1)$, and the agent only contracts with principal 2. The agent gets no rent in this equilibrium.*

It is interesting to compare Example B.1 with the results of Proposition 5. In this case, free riding was limited to some players offering a null contribution. With unrestricted contracting but enough heterogeneity among principals, free riding is such that inactive players offer out-of-equilibrium contributions that force the other principals to reduce their own contributions compared to what they would do were these other players absent.[6]

Yet, the results here share the common feature with those in Section 6. Partial participation will be more likely to emerge as the degree of heterogeneity among principals increases.

Proofs

Proof of Proposition B.1. Note first that (B.2) is necessarily binding at the optimum of (P_i^D). Otherwise, principal i could increase C_i. Moreover, for all i, the constraint is binding either with the r.h.s. being equal to 0, either with the maximum being reached for some S^* such that $i \notin S^*$. Otherwise, principal i could again increase C_i. Inserting the corresponding value of the fee C_i into the objective function of the agent leads therefore to maximize with respect to a_i an expression including

$$(b_i - a_i)a_N + \frac{(1 - r\sigma^2)}{2}a_N^2$$

plus some constant terms. The first-order condition with respect to a_i yields

$$b_i = a_i^D + r\sigma^2 a_N. \tag{B.6}$$

From which we derive

$$a_N^D = \frac{B_N}{1 + nr\sigma^2}$$

---

[6] If more than one principal offer negative piece rates, the equilibrium will be such that one principal remains inactive while proposing a deterring contract. This contract prevents principals with a positive piece rate to increase this rate, making the deviation to a smaller coalition impossible. Generically, if all valuations are different, all equilibria will entail all principals but one being active, some of them potentially offering negative piece rates.

and thus (B.4). Assumption (B.3) ensures that for all $i \in N$, $0 \geq a_i \geq b_i$, so that there is no loss of generality in assuming interior solutions as we do.

Note that the effort supplied by the agent is always positive and can be rewritten

$$e = \frac{B_N}{1 + nr\sigma^2}.$$

With (B.4), we can write

$$a_S^D = B_S - \frac{r\sigma^2 |S|}{1 + nr\sigma^2} B_N.$$

The vector of fixed fees $(C_i^D)_{1 \leq i \leq n}$ solves then the system

$$\frac{(1 - r\sigma^2)}{2} \left(B_N - \frac{nr\sigma^2}{1 + nr\sigma^2} B_N \right)^2 - C_N^D \tag{B.7}$$

$$= \max \left\{ 0, \max_{S \subset N} \left\{ \frac{(1 - r\sigma^2)}{2} \left(B_S - \frac{r\sigma^2 |S|}{1 + nr\sigma^2} B_N \right)^2 - C_S^D \right\} \right\}.$$

Assumption (B.3) guarantees that for all i, $a_i \geq 0$, and that $B_S - \frac{r\sigma^2 |S|}{1 + nr\sigma^2} B_N \geq 0$. Consider now the following system

$$C_N^D = \frac{(1 - r\sigma^2)}{2} \left(B_N - \frac{nr\sigma^2}{1 + nr\sigma^2} B_N \right)^2, \tag{B.8}$$

$$C_S^D \leq \frac{(1 - r\sigma^2)}{2} \left\{ \left(B_N - \frac{nr\sigma^2}{1 + nr\sigma^2} B_N \right)^2 \right.$$

$$\left. - \left(B_{N-S} - \frac{r\sigma^2 |N - S|}{1 + nr\sigma^2} B_N \right)^2 \right\} \quad \forall S \subset N. \tag{B.9}$$

Proceeding as in the proof of Proposition 2, assuming that $1 > r\sigma^2$ and that (B.3) holds, this system has a solution when

$$\left(B_N - \frac{nr\sigma^2}{1 + nr\sigma^2} B_N \right)^2 \geq \left(B_S - \frac{r\sigma^2 |S|}{1 + nr\sigma^2} B_N \right)^2$$

$$+ \left(B_{N-S} - \frac{r\sigma^2 |N - S|}{1 + nr\sigma^2} B_N \right)^2 \quad \forall S \subset N. \tag{B.10}$$

That x^2 is convex guarantees that the cooperative game with characteristic form

$$\tilde{W}_S = \left(B_S - \frac{r\sigma^2 |S|}{1 + nr\sigma^2} B_N \right)^2$$

is itself convex. It has thus a nonempty core. From this, it follows that the agent makes zero payoff in any equilibrium where all principals are active and that the solutions to (B.8) and (B.9) exist.[7]

The Grand-Coalition Emerges. We must check that no principal wants to induce another active coalition than N. For this to be true, we must have for each i:

$$N - \{i\} = \arg \max_{S \subseteq N - \{i\}} \left\{ \max_a \left\{ (b_i - a)(a + a_S^D) + \frac{(1 - r\sigma^2)}{2}(a + a_S^D)^2 - C_S^D \right\} \right\}$$

(B.11)

where the expression in the maximand is what principal i gets by inducing an active coalition of principals $S \cup \{i\}$, up to some constant terms which are worth

$$U_R = \max \left\{ 0, \max_{K \subset N} \left\{ \frac{(1 - r\sigma^2)}{2}(a_K^D)^2 - C_K^D \right\} \right\}.$$

The optimal response to the piece rate a_S^D is thus to charge a piece rate

$$a_i = \frac{b_i - r\sigma^2 a_S^D}{1 + r\sigma^2}.$$

Condition (B.11) can then be written as:

$$\frac{(b_i + a_{-i}^D)^2}{2(1 + r\sigma^2)} - C_{-i}^D \geq \frac{(b_i + a_S^D)^2}{2(1 + r\sigma^2)} - C_S^D \quad \forall S \subseteq N - \{i\}.$$

(B.12)

Taking into account that, from (B.4),

$$a_S^D = B_S - \frac{r\sigma^2|S|}{1 + n r\sigma^2} B_N,$$

(B.12) holds when

$$\frac{1}{2(1 + r\sigma^2)} \left(\left(B_N - \frac{r\sigma^2(n - 1)}{1 + n r\sigma^2} B_N \right)^2 - \left(B_S - \frac{r\sigma^2(|S| - 1)}{1 + n r\sigma^2} B_N \right)^2 \right) \geq C_{N-S}^D$$

(B.13)

for all $S \subseteq N$.[8]

But, from (B.8) and (B.9),

$$C_{N-S} \leq \frac{(1 - r\sigma^2)}{2} \left[\left(B_N - \frac{n r\sigma^2}{1 + n r\sigma^2} B_N \right)^2 - \left(B_S - \frac{r\sigma^2|S|}{1 + n r\sigma^2} B_N \right)^2 \right].$$

---

[7] Note that the cooperative game with characteristic form $\tilde{W}_S$ is no longer convex for $1 \leq r\sigma^2$.

[8] The sufficient condition is that this condition holds for all $S \subseteq N$ such that $|S| \geq 1$.

Hence, (B.13) holds when the following sufficient condition holds:

$$(1 - r\sigma^2)(1 + r\sigma^2)\left[\left(B_N - \frac{nr\sigma^2}{1 + nr\sigma^2}B_N\right)^2 - \left(B_S - \frac{r\sigma^2|S|}{1 + nr\sigma^2}B_N\right)^2\right] \quad (B.14)$$

$$\leq \left[\left(B_N - \frac{(n-1)r\sigma^2}{1 + nr\sigma^2}B_N\right)^2 - \left(B_S - \frac{r\sigma^2(|S| - 1)}{1 + nr\sigma^2}B_N\right)^2\right] \text{ for any } S \subset N.$$

A weaker sufficient condition is

$$\left(B_N - \frac{nr\sigma^2}{1 + nr\sigma^2}B_N\right)^2 - \left(B_S - \frac{r\sigma^2|S|}{1 + nr\sigma^2}B_N\right)^2 \quad (B.15)$$

$$\leq \left[\left(B_N - \frac{(n-1)r\sigma^2}{1 + nr\sigma^2}B_N\right)^2 - \left(B_S - \frac{r\sigma^2(|S| - 1)}{1 + nr\sigma^2}B_N\right)^2\right] \text{ for any } S \subset N.$$

Observing that this condition can be written as

$$A^2 - B^2 \leq C^2 - D^2,$$

with $A - B = C - D \geq 0$ (from Assumption (B.3)) and $A + B \leq C + D$, this is always true.

No Other Equilibrium with a Proper Coalition of Active Principals Exists

Let suppose that an equilibrium with a proper coalition of active principals A^* forms. Let a_{A^*} be the aggregate piece rate offered by those principals to the agent and C_{A^*} the aggregate fixed fee. The agent's effort is thus a_{A^*} and his certainty equivalent payoff from accepting this aggregate scheme:

$$U_{A^*} = \frac{(1 - r\sigma^2)}{2}a_{A^*}^2 - C_{A^*}.$$

Let $i_0 \notin A^*$. Principal i_0 gets an expected payoff $b_{i_0}a_{A^*}$ since his offer is rejected by the agent.

Consider now the following deviation by principal i_0 which consists in offering a piece rate $a_{i_0} \in (0, b_i)$ and a fixed fee $C_{i_0} > 0$ so that the agent is indifferent between contracting with the coalition A^* and with $A^* \cup \{i_0\}$. Accepting this new contract and all offers from A^* gives the agent at least U_{A^*}.

As in the Proof of Proposition 2, two cases have to be considered:

1. *First case:* The agent accepts exactly the offers of principals in $A^* \cup \{i_0\}$.
   He exerts now effort $a_{i_0} + a_{A^*}$ and principal i_0 gets an expected payoff

$$(b_{i_0} - a_{i_0})(a_{i_0} + a_{A^*}) + \frac{(1 - r\sigma^2)}{2}(a_{i_0} + a_{A^*}^2) - C_{A^*} - U_{A^*}.$$

Maximizing this expression with respect to a_{i_0} gives an expected payoff to principal i_0 which is strictly greater than what he gets when his offer is rejected (indeed, this latter payoff is obtained when $a_{i_0} = 0$ in the preceding expression). Hence, principal i_0 has a valuable deviation which invalidates an equilibrium with only a proper coalition of principals being active.

2. *Second case:* The introduction of the fixed fee a_{i_0}, by increasing the agent's effort, leads him to accept other contracts that he previously refused, and possibly to refuse some contracts he used to accept. Let us denote S^* the new set of principals different from i_0 whose contracts are accepted by the agent. It is not necessary a priori that $A^* \subseteq S^*$. Yet, we make use of the fact that contracts (even out of equilibrium) are restricted to be linear.

The important point is to show that such a recombination of accepted contracts can only increase the effort, that is,

$$a_{i_0} + a_{S^*} \geq a_{i_0} + a_{A^*}.$$

We prove this result in two steps.

- The first step is to recognize that for A^* to be an equilibrium, the agent must contract with i_0 in any possible deviation.
- The second step is to notice that for the agent to prefer to contract with principals in $S^* \cup \{i_0\}$, it must be that

$$\frac{1 - r\sigma^2}{2} \left(a_{A^*} + a_{i_0}\right)^2 - C_{A^*} - C_{i_0} \leq \frac{1 - r\sigma^2}{2} \left(a_{S^*} + a_{i_0}\right)^2 - C_{S^*} - C_{i_0},$$

or again

$$\frac{1 - r\sigma^2}{2} \left[a_{A^*}^2 + 2a_{i_0}a_{A^*}\right] - C_{A^*} \leq \frac{1 - r\sigma^2}{2} \left[a_{S^*}^2 + 2a_{i_0}a_{S^*}\right] - C_{S^*}.$$

But since A^* is part of an equilibrium

$$\frac{1 - r\sigma^2}{2} a_{A^*}^2 - C_{A^*} \geq \frac{1 - r\sigma^2}{2} a_{S^*}^2 - C_{S^*}.$$

Therefore, a condition for the agent now to prefer S^* to A^* is

$$a_{A^*} \leq a_{S^*}$$

Notice now that principal i_0 gets an expected payoff

$$(b_{i_0} - a_{i_0})(a_{S^*} + a_{i_0}) + C_{i_0}.$$

This payoff is larger than when $S^* = A^*$, making a deviation in this case still more valuable. There is no equilibrium with only a proper coalition of principals being active. □

Proof of Proposition B.2. When Assumption (B.3) does not hold, some principals will offer a negative piece rate (and therefore a negative fixed fee as well). The condition for the agent to accept all contracts becomes

$$\frac{(1-r\sigma^2)}{2}a_N^2 - C_N \geq \max\left\{0, \max_{S \subset N} U_S\right\},\tag{B.16}$$

where

$$U_S = \begin{cases} \frac{(1-r\sigma^2)}{2}a_S^2 - C_S \text{ if } a_S \geq 0 \\ \frac{-r\sigma^2}{2}a_S^2 - C_S \text{ if } a_S < 0, \end{cases}$$

the last line coming from the fact that proposed with a negative aggregate piece rate the agent will choose $e = 0$.

Let us show that there cannot be an equilibrium where all principals are active. To do so, we proceed in two steps.

- *Deviation in case the agent gets some rent.* First, we show that as soon as the agent gets some rent, there is a deviation from the putative equilibrium where all principals are active.

  If the agent gets some rent, then for all $i \in N$, there exists S with $i \notin S$ such that (B.16) is binding for S. In particular, choosing i such that $a_i > 0$, and denoting a_S the aggregate piece rate, there exists S^* with $a_{S^*} > a_N$ such that (B.16) is binding for S^*.

  Consider principal $i_0 \in S^*$ with $a_{i_0} > 0$. By raising a_{i_0} marginally, principal i_0 induces the agent to prefer offers by S^* only. Indeed, since $a_{S^*} > a_N \geq 0$,

  $$\frac{\partial U_S}{\partial a_{i_0}} > \frac{\partial U_N}{\partial a_{i_0}}.$$

  The agent may as well prefer now another sub-coalition $\tilde{S}$, but it will still be the case that $a_{\tilde{S}} > a_N$.

  The payoff of principal i_0 when he proposes this new contract becomes

  $$(b_{i_0} - a_{i_0})a_{\tilde{S}} - C_{i_0}.$$

  While the increase in a_{i_0} is infinitesimal, the increase in $a_{\tilde{S}}$ is not. This deviation is therefore profitable for principal i_0.

- *Existence of a rent for the agent.* We denote S^+ the set of principals that offer a non negative piece rate, and S^- the set of those offering a negative piece rate. Let n^+ and n^- be their respective cardinals. With transparent notations, $a^\pm$ and $B^\pm$ are the sum of contributions and valuations of those two subsets, and $C^\pm$ the aggregated fixed fees.

Let us assume that the agent gets no rent. In this case

$$\frac{1 - r\sigma^2}{2} \left(a^+ + a^-\right)^2 - C^+ - C^- = 0. \tag{B.17}$$

By accepting only all offers in S^+, the agent can get a payoff $U^+ = \frac{1 - r\sigma^2}{2} (a^+)^2 - C^+$. By accepting only all offers in S^-, he gets a payoff $U^+ = -\frac{r\sigma^2}{2} (a^-)^2 - C^-$. Summing these two terms while using (B.17), we find

$$U^+ + U_- = (-a^-) \left[(1 - r\sigma^2)a^+ + \frac{1}{2}a^- \right].$$

It is clear that the sign of this expression is positive when $r\sigma^2 \leq \frac{1}{2}$. On the other hand, it is negative in the extreme case when $r\sigma^2 = 1$. The result follows. $\qquad\square$

Proof of Example B.1. Let $n = 2$, $b_1 = 1$, $b_2 = 5$, $r\sigma^2 = \frac{1}{2}$. We first identify the characteristic of a putative equilibrium where both principals are active. We then show that such an equilibrium cannot exist because principal 2 wants to deviate. We eventually construct an equilibrium where only principal 2 is active.

When Both Principals Are Active. In this case, the piece rates they offer are still determined by (B.6). Therefore, $a_1 = -\frac{1}{2}$ and $a_2 = \frac{7}{2}$.

We can apply the idea of (B.5), being careful to the fact that if the agent contracts with only principal 1 his optimal effort will have a corner solution, $e = 0$, with an associated certainty-equivalent payoff $-\frac{1}{4}(a_1)^2 - C_1 = -\frac{1}{16} - C_1$.

The condition for the agent to accept both offers is therefore

$$\frac{9}{4} - C_1 - C_2 \geq \max\{0, -\frac{1}{16} - C_1, \frac{49}{16} - C_2\}.$$

The solutions (C_1, C_2) are the solutions to the system

$$C_1 + C_2 \leq \frac{9}{4},$$

$$C_1 \leq -\frac{13}{16} \text{ and}$$

$$C_2 \leq \frac{37}{16}. \tag{B.18}$$

Notice that $\frac{37}{16} - \frac{13}{16} = \frac{3}{2} < \frac{9}{4}$: the constraint $C_1 + C_2 \leq \frac{9}{4}$ will not be binding.

It follows that there is a unique solution to the system,

$$C_1 = -\frac{13}{16} \text{ and } C_2 = \frac{37}{16}. \tag{B.19}$$

The agent gets a positive rent, with an associated payoff equal to $\frac{3}{4}$. This payoff is the same whether he contracts with both principals or only one of them.

Deviation by Principal 2. It is easy to check that principal 1 has no profitable deviation.

Instead, principal 2 does have an incentive to form a proper coalition with the agent, excluding principal 1.

Such an exclusive contracting will be possible with a contract $(\tilde{a}_2, \tilde{C}_2)$ such that

$$\frac{1}{4}\tilde{a}_2^2 - \tilde{C}_2 \geq \frac{3}{4} \text{ (the agent does not prefer the contract with}$$

principal 1 alone) and

$$\frac{1}{4}(\tilde{a}_2 - \frac{1}{2})^2 - \tilde{C}_2 + \frac{13}{16} \geq \frac{1}{4}\tilde{a}_2^2 - C_2 \text{ (the agent does not prefer to}$$

contract with both.

The second condition amounts to $a_2 \geq \frac{7}{2}$.

By choosing $\tilde{a}_2 = \frac{7}{2} + \epsilon$, with $\epsilon > 0$ arbitrarily small, and $\tilde{C}_2 = \frac{1}{4}\tilde{a}_2^2 - \frac{3}{4}$, that can be made arbitrarily close from $\frac{37}{16}$, principal 2 can induce the agent to refuse the offer by principal 1.[9]

Such a deviation would ensure him a payoff of $(5 - \frac{7}{2})\frac{7}{2} + \frac{37}{16} = \frac{12}{16}$. The payoff before the deviation was $(5 - \frac{7}{2}) \times 3 + \frac{37}{16} = \frac{109}{16}$. The deviation is profitable. There is therefore no equilibrium with both groups having their contracts accepted.

Equilibrium Where Only Principal 2 Is Active: Consider the following candidate equilibrium: $(a_2, C_2) = (2, 1)$ and $(a_1, C_1) = (-10, -17)$, while the agent only accepts the offer by principal 2.

The agent is indifferent between accepting the offer of principal 2, refusing all offers, and refusing both offers. We break this indifference with the agent accepting only the offer of principal 2. This brings principal 2 an expected payoff of 7.

Let us check that principal 2 has no profitable deviation.

Principal 2 would like to increase a_2, but without inducing principal 1 to accept both offers. However, this is marginally impossible, since the condition for the agent not to do so is

$$\frac{1}{4}a_2^2 - C_1 \geq -\frac{1}{4}(a_1 + a_2)^2 - C_1 - C_2.$$

$$\Leftrightarrow \frac{1}{2}a_2^2 - 5a_2 + 8 \geq 0.$$

This inequality is only satisfied for $a_2 \leq 2$ or $a_2 \geq 8$. Remember that when alone, principal 2 would choose $a_2 = \frac{10}{3} < 8$. Therefore, to deter the agent from

---

[9] It can be easily checked that this is the optimal deviation by principal 2, since absent any constraint he would choose $a_2 = \frac{10}{3} < \frac{7}{2}$.

accepting both offers, principal 2 will optimally choose $a_2 = 8$. C_2 is determined by $-\frac{1}{4}a_2^2 - C_2 \geq 0$, that leads to $C_2 = 16$.[10] But the payoff of principal 2 is then $(5 - 8) \times 8 + 16 = -8$.

Principal 2 could also propose a contract such that the agent accepts both offers. In this case, the effort by the agent would be $e = \max\{0, a_2 - 10\}$. If $e > 0$, the payoff of principal 2 is quadratic and maximized for $a_2 = \frac{10-a_1}{3} = \frac{20}{3} < 10$. This means that the constraint $e \geq 0$ will be binding.

The binding constraint for C_2 will be the one stipulating that the agent should not prefer to refuse both offers, which gives $C_2 \leq -\frac{1}{4}(a_2 - 10)^2 - 17$. The expected payoff of principal 2 is thus given by $-\frac{1}{4}(a_2 - 10)^2 - 17$. It reaches its maximum in $a_2 = 10$, and gives a negative payoff.

Principal 2 therefore has no profitable deviation.

No Equilibrium Where Only Principal 1 Is Active. For an equilibrium where only principal 1 is active to exist, it must be that $a_2^*(a_1) = \frac{10-a_1}{3} = 0$. But for $a_1 = 10$, a condition for the agent to accept the contract is $\frac{10^2}{4} - C_1 \geq 0$. The payoff of principal 1 is therefore smaller that $(1 - 10) \times 10 + 25 < 0$. Principal 1 will prefer not to offer any contract, or at least to reduce the piece rate (this is possible if $a_2 < 0$. If $a_2 \geq 0$, then whatever the agent's reaction to $a_1 = 0$, principal 1 would be better of with such a deviation). $\square$

---

[10] The constraint that the agent does not prefer to contract with principal 1 alone is in this case $C_2 \leq 24$.

References

Aidt, T. (1998). "Political Internalization of Economic Externallities and Environmental Policy," *Journal of Public Economics*, 69: 1–16.

Arnott, R. and J. Stiglitz (1991). "Equilibrium in Competitive Insurance Markets with Moral Hazard," NBER Working Paper 3588.

Attar, A., C. Casamatta, A. Chassagnon and J. P. Décamps (2019). "Multiple Lenders, Strategic Default and Covenants," *American Economic Journal: Microeconomics,* 11: 98–130.

Attar, A. and A. Chassagnon (2009). "On Moral Hazard and Nonexclusive Contracts," *Journal of Mathematical Economics,* 45: 511–525.

Attar, A., G. Piaser and N. Porteiro (2007a). "Negotiation and Take-It or Leave-It in Common Agency with Non-Contractible Actions," *Journal of Economic Theory,* 135: 590–593.

Attar, A., G. Piaser and N. Porteiro (2007b). "A Note on Common Agency Models of Moral Hazard," *Economics Letters,* 95: 278–284.

Aumann, R. J. (1959). "Acceptable Points in General Cooperative n-Person Games," in A. W. Tucker and R. D. Luce, eds., *Contributions to the Theory of Games IV,* Princeton University Press, Princeton, 287–324.

Baron, D. (1985). "Noncooperative Regulation of a Nonlocalized Externality," *The RAND Journal of Economics,* 16: 553–568.

Becker, G. (1983). "A Theory of Competition Among Pressure Groups for Political Influence," *Quarterly Journal of Economics*, 98: 371–400.

Becker, G. (1985). "Public Policies, Pressure Groups and Dead-Weight Costs," *Journal of Public Economics*, 28: 329–346.

Bentley, A. (1908). *The Process of Government,* University of Chicago Press, Chicago.

Bergstrom, T., L. Blume and H. Varian (1986). "On the Private Provision of Public Goods," *Journal of Public Economics*, 29: 25–49.

Bernheim, D. (1986). "On the Voluntary and Involuntary Provision of Public Goods," *American Economic Review*, 76: 789–793.

Bernheim, B., B. Peleg and M. Whinston (1987). "Coalition-Proof Nash Equilibria I. Concepts," *Journal of Economic Theory,* 42: 1–12.

Bernheim, D. and M. Whinston (1986a). "Common Agency," *Econometrica,* 54: 923–942.

Bernheim, D. and M. Whinston (1986b). "Menu Auctions, Resource Allocations and Economic Influence," *Quarterly Journal of Economics*, 101: 1–31.

Besley, T. and S. Coate (2001). "Lobbying and Welfare in a Representative Democracy," *The Review of Economic Studies*, 68: 67–82.

Bisin, A. and D. Guaitoli (2004). "Moral Hazard and Nonexclusive Contracts," *The RAND Journal of Economics*, 35: 306–328.

Bombardini, M. (2008). "Firm Heterogeneity and Lobby Participation," *Journal of International Economics*, 75: 329–348.

Chiesa, G. and V. Denicolò (2009). "Trading with a Common Agent under Complete Information: A Characterization of Nash Equilibria," *Journal of Economic Theory*, 144: 296–311.

Clarke, E. (1971). "Multipart Pricing of Public Goods," *Public Choice*, 11: 19–33.

Dahl, R. (1961). *Who Governs? Democracy and Power in an American City*, Yale University Press, New Heaven, London.

Dixit, A. (1996). *The Making of Economic Policy*, MIT Press, Cambridge, MA.

Dixit, A., G. Grossman and E. Helpman (1997). "Common Agency and Coordination: General Theory and Application to Government Policy Making," *Journal of Political Economy*, 105: 752–769.

Epstein, D. and S. O'Halloran (1997). "Modelling Madison: A Multiple Principals Model of Interest Groups Competition," Harvard University mimeo.

Epstein, D. and S. O'Halloran (1999). *Delegating Powers: A Transaction Cost Politics Approach to Policy Making under Separate Powers*, Cambridge University Press, Cambridge.

Fraysse, J. (1993). "Common Agency: Existence of an Equilibrium in the Case of Two Outcomes," *Econometrica*, 61: 1225–1229.

Furusawa, T. and H. Konishi (2011). "Contributing or Free-Riding? Voluntary Participation in a Public Good Economy," *Theoretical Economics*, 6: 29–256.

Gottlieb, D. and H. Moreira (2022). "Simple Contracts with Adverse Selection and Moral Hazard," *Theoretical Economics*, 17(3): 1357–1401.

Green, J. and J. J. Laffont (1977). "Characterization of Satisfactory Mechanisms for the Revelation of Preferences for Public Goods," *Econometrica*, 45: 427–438.

Grossman, S. and O. Hart (1983). "An Analysis of the Principal-Agent Problem," *Econometrica*, 51: 7–46.

Grossman, G. and E. Helpman (1994). "Protection for Sale," *American Economic Review*, 84: 833–850.

Grossman, G. and E. Helpman (2001). *Special Interest Politics*, MIT Press, Cambridge, MA.

Groves, T. (1973). "Incentives in Teams," *Econometrica*, 41: 617–631.

Hellwig, M. (1983). "On Moral Hazard and Non-price Equilibria in Competitive Insurance Markets," mimeo.

Hellwig, M. (2003). "Public-Good Provision with Many Participants," *The Review of Economic Studies*, 70: 589–614.

Helpman, E. and J. J. Laffont (1975). "On Moral Hazard in General Equilibrium," *Journal of Economic Theory*, 10: 8–23.

Helpman, E. and T. Persson (2001). "Lobbying and Legislative Bargaining," *Advances in Economic Analysis and Policy*, 1(1): 1–33.

Holmstrom, B. (1979). "Moral Hazard and Observability," *The Bell Journal of Economics*, 10(1): 74–91.

Holmstrom, B. and P. Milgrom (1987). "Aggregation and Linearity in the Provision of Intertemporal Incentives," *Econometrica*, 55: 303–328.

Hula, K. (1999). *Lobbying Together: Interest Group Coalitions in Legislative Politics*, Georgetown University Press, Washington DC.

Kahn, C. and D. Mookherjee (1995). "Coalition Proof Equilibrium in an Adverse Selection Insurance Economy," *Journal of Economic Theory*, 66: 113–138.

Kiewiet, R. and M. McCubbins (1991). *The Logic of Delegation*, University of Chicago Press, Chicago.

Kirchsteiger, G. and A. Prat (2001). "Inefficient Equilibria in Lobbying," *Journal of Public Economics*, 82: 349–375.

Laffont, J. J. and D. Martimort (2002). *The Theory of Incentives: The Principal-Agent Model,* Princeton University Press, Princeton.

Laussel, D. and M. Le Breton (1998a). "Efficient Private Production of Public Goods under Common Agency," *Games and Economic Behavior*, 25: 194–218.

Laussel, D. and M. Le Breton (1998b). "Free Riding as a By-Product of Incentive Constraints: A New Look at the Private Provision of Public Goods," Mimeo GREQAM, Université de la Méditerranée.

Laussel, D. and M. Le Breton (2001). "Conflict and Cooperation: The Structure of Equilibrium Payoffs in Common Agency," *Journal of Economic Theory*, 100: 93–128.

Le Breton, M. and F. Salanié (2003). "Lobbying under Political Uncertainty," *Journal of Public Economics*, 87: 2589–2610.

Leaver, C. and M. Makris (2006). "Passive Industry Interests in Large Polity," *Journal of Public Economic Theory*, 8: 571–602.

Lefebvre, P. and D. Martimort (2020). "When Olson Meets Dahl': From Inefficient Groups Formation to Inefficient Policy-Making," *The Journal of Politics*, 82: 1026–1043.

Lima, R. and H. Moreira (2014). "Information Transmission and Inefficient Lobbying," *Games and Economic Behavior*, 86: 282–307.

Mailath, G. and A. Postlewaite (1990). "Asymmetric Information Bargaining Problems with Many Agents," *The Review of Economic Studies*, 57: 351–367.

Mallard, G. (2014). "Static Common Agency and Political Influence: An Evaluative Survey," *Journal of Economic Surveys*, 28: 17–35.

Martimort, D. (1996). "The Multi-Principal Nature of the Government," *European Economic Review*, 40: 673–685.

Martimort, D. (2007). "Multi-Contracting Mechanism Design," in R. Blundell, W. K. Newey, and T. Persson, eds., *Advances in Economic Theory Proceedings of the World Congress of the Econometric Society*, Cambridge University Press, Cambridge, UK.

Martimort, D. (2018). "Une revue critique de la théorie de l'agence commune appliquée aux jeux de lobbies," *Revue Économique*, 69: 1025–1053.

Martimort, D. and H. Moreira (2010). "Common Agency and Public Good Provision under Asymmetric Information," *Theoretical Economics*, 5: 159–213.

Martimort, D. and A. Semenov (2007a). "The Pluralistic View of Politics: Asymmetric Lobbyists, Ideological Uncertainty and Political Entry," *Economics Letters*, 97: 155–161.

Martimort, D. and A. Semenov (2007b). "Political Biases in Lobbying under Asymmetric Information," *Journal of the European Economic Association*, 5: 614–623.

Martimort, D. and A. Semenov (2008). "Ideological Uncertainty and Lobbying Competition," *Journal of Public Economics*, 92: 456–481.

Martimort, D. and L. Stole (2003). "Contractual Externalities and Common Agency Equilibria," *Advances in Theoretical Economics*, 3(1): Article 4. www.bepress.com/bejte.

Martimort, D. and L. Stole (2009). "Selecting Equilibria in Common Agency Games," *Journal of Economic Theory*, 144: 604–634.

Martimort, D. and L. Stole (2012). "Representing Equilibrium Aggregates in Aggregate Games with Applications to Common Agency," *Games and Economic Behavior*, 76: 753–772.

Martimort, D. and L. Stole (2018). "Menu Auctions and Influence Games with Private Information," SSRN 2569703. https://ssrn.com/abstract=2569703

Mirrlees, J. (1999). "The Theory of Moral Hazard and Unobservable Behaviour: Part I," *The Review of Economic Studies*, 66: 3–21.

Mirrlees, J. (1976). "The Optimal Structure of Incentives and Authority within an Organization." *The Bell Journal of Economics*. 7:105–131.

Mitra, D. (1999). "Endogenous Lobby Formation and Endogenous Protection: A Long-Run Model of Trade Policy Formation," *American Economic Review*, 89: 1116–1134.

Moe, T. (1981). *The Organization of Interests*, University of Chicago, Chicago.

Moe, T. (1989). "The Politics of Structural Choice: Towards a Theory of Public Bureaucracy," in O. Williamson, ed., *Organization Theory: From Chester Barnard to the Present and Beyond*, Oxford University Press, Oxford, 116–153.

Olson, M. (1965). *The Logic of Collective Action*, Harvard University Press, Boston.

Pauly, M. (1974). "Overprovision and Public Provision of Insurance: The Roles of Adverse Selection and Moral Hazard," *The Quarterly Journal of Economics,* 88: 44–62.

Peltzman, S. (1976). "Toward a More General Theory of Regulation," *The Journal of Law and Economics*, 19: 211–240.

Peters, M. (2003). "Negotiation and Take It or Leave it in Common Agency," *Journal of Economic Theory,* 111: 88–109.

Peters, M. and B. Szentes (2012). "Definable and Contractible Contracts," *Econometrica,* 80: 363–411.

Rama, M. and G. Tabellini (1998). "Lobbying by Capital and Labor Overtrade and Labor Market Policies," *European Economic Review*, 42: 1296–1316.

Ray, D. and R. Vohra (1997). "Equilibrium Binding Agreements," *Journal of Economic Theory*, 73: 30–78.

Shapley, L. (1971). "Cores of Convex Games," *International Journal of Game Theory*, 1: 11–26.

Snyder, J. and B. Weingast (2000). "The American System of Shared Powers: The President, Congress, and the NLRB," *Journal of Law, Economics and Organization,* 16: 269–305.

Spiller, P. and S. Urbiztondo (1994). "Political Appointees vs. Career Civil Servants: A Multiple Principals Theory of Political Bureaucracies," *European Journal of Political Economy*, 10: 465–497.

Szentes, B. (2015). "Contractible Contracts in Common Agency Problems," *The Review of Economic Studies,* 82: 391–422.

Truman, D. (1951). *The Government Process*, Knopf, New York.

Warr, P. (1983). "The Private Provision of a Public Good is Independent of the Distribution of Income," *Economics Letters,* 13: 207–211.

Wilson, J. (1989). *Bureaucracy*, Basic Books, New York.

Yu, Z. (2005). "Environmental Protection: A Theory of Direct and Indirect Competition for Political Influence," *The Review of Economic Studies*, 72: 269–286.

Acknowledgements

An earlier version of this Element was circulated under the title "Delegated Common Agency under Moral Hazard and the Formation of Interest Groups". We thank Michel Le Breton and Wilfried Sand-Zantman for useful and continuing discussions on the topic of this Element. This Element also benefited from comments by seminar participants at the University of Namur. Part of this research was completed while the second author was visiting Toulouse School of Economics, which is thanked for its hospitality and for financial support from the ERC (MARKLIN). The usual disclaimer applies.

Acknowledgement

Cambridge Elements ☰

Law, Economics and Politics

Series Editor in Chief
Carmine Guerriero, *University of Bologna*

Series Co-Editors
Alessandro Riboni, *École Polytechnique*
Jillian Grennan, *Duke University, Fuqua School of Business*
Petros Sekeris, *Montpellier Business School*

Series Managing Editor
Valentino Moscariello, *University of Bologna*

Series Associate Editors
Maija Halonen-Akatwijuka, *University of Bristol*
Sara Biancini, *Université de Cergy-Pontoise*
Melanie Meng Xue, *London School of Economics and Political Science*
Claire Lim, *Queen Mary University of London*
Andy Hanssen, *Clemson University*
Giacomo Benati, *Eberhard Karls University, Tübingen*

About the Series
Decisions taken by individuals are influenced by formal and informal institutions. Legal and political institutions determine the nature, scope and operation of markets, organisations, and states. This interdisciplinary series analyses the functioning, determinants, and impact of these institutions, organizing the existing knowledge and guiding future research.

Cambridge Elements $\equiv$

Law, Economics and Politics

Elements in the Series

The Strategic Analysis of Judicial Behavior: A Comparative Perspective
Lee Epstein and Keren Weinshall

Can Blockchain Solve the Hold-up Problem in Contracts?
Richard Holden and Anup Malani

Deep IV in Law: Appellate Decisions and Texts Impact Sentencing in Trial Courts
Zhe Huang, Xinyue Zhang, Ruofan Wang, and Daniel L. Chen

Reform for Sale
Perrin Lefebvre and David Martimort

Printed in the United States
by Baker & Taylor Publisher Services